THE
UNHAPPY
GAYS

Tim LaHaye

THE UNHAPPY GAYS

What everyone should know about homosexuality

TYNDALE HOUSE
PUBLISHERS, INC.
WHEATON, ILLINOIS

Library of Congress Catalog
Card Number 77-93751
ISBN 0-8423-7797-2
Copyright © 1978 by
Tim LaHaye.
First printing, June 1978
Printed in the United States
of America.

CONTENTS

The Homosexual Explosion

Something strange is going on in America! My wife and I had been out of the country only nine months, holding family life seminars in forty-two countries around the world, but we noticed it immediately. Arriving in San Diego on a Sunday, I looked through my mail and found two letters from lesbians and four from homosexuals. That day the first reports of the "trash-can murders" hit the press, announcing the sadistic murders of as many as twenty-four homosexuals. We left the next day to attend the Christian Booksellers Convention, where both our new books were released. On Wednesday night, while walking to the auditorium to hear Anita Bryant interviewed on a television show, I was startled by a shouting crowd of gays bearing placards featuring such slogans as "Gay Rights Now," "God Loves Gays, Too, Anita," and "Gay Is Good." I could hardly believe the security measures required backstage to guarantee Miss Bryant's protection.

While winding up our tour in the Orient, I had read about the defeat Miss Bryant and her friends in Dade County had administered to the gay community and how demonstrations of angry gays appeared almost overnight in New York City, San Francisco, and many other parts of the country.

Subsequent press stories indicated that everywhere Miss
Bryant appeared, she was harassed by a gay demonstration.

My head was still spinning from all this when Wendell
Hawley of Tyndale House remarked, "The Christian
community needs a penetrating book on homosexuality. Why
don't you write it?" My first reaction was, "I'll pray about
it." I didn't have to wait long for an answer, for everywhere
I turned I seemed to be confronted with someone who was a
homosexual or knew one. When I mentioned Dr. Hawley's
observation to my pilot friend, who shared flying chores with
me on the flight home, he replied, "My wife's brother
announced recently that he was gay." The morning after our
return, the San Diego *Union* carried the story of a former
police sergeant who had just announced that he had been gay
during the ten years he had served on the police force.
Apparently our local chief had angered him by suggesting that
a gay couldn't do police work, so he publicized his past and
called attention to his impeccable police record. The story was
carried that evening on nationwide television.

A few days later, while conducting a seminar on counseling
for ministers in a northern California city, I was urged by
one of the pastors to talk with a lady in his congregation. She
turned out to be an attractive thirty-two-year-old mother of
three, married for ten years, who thanked me for the help she
had gained some years ago from one of my books. Almost
immediately she burst into tears. "My husband just
informed me he is gay!" It turned out that this gifted concert
violinist knew a great deal about gays, for she lamented,
"I'm surrounded by them in our city orchestra—the director
and over half of the musicians prefer men to women!"

Everywhere I turned, newspapers, television, and many
individuals bombarded me with the realization that America is
experiencing a homosexual epidemic.

It Isn't New

Homosexuality is almost as old as man. The first mention in recorded history concerns Lot and the well-known cities of Sodom and Gomorrah, over 4000 years ago. The Bible tells in graphic detail how the men of Sodom tried to sexually molest the angelic messengers of God, who looked like men, as they came to warn Lot to flee the city before its impending destruction. The word *sodomy* (men practicing sex with men) has become a byword for homosexuality and is obviously derived from that ancient city.

Although the widespread practice of incest among Egyptian pharaohs is well documented by historians, some confirm that homosexuality was also common among them. By the 8th century B.C., the prophet Isaiah spoke out against the leaders of Israel just before their captivity, warning that they had incurred the wrath of God because they not only practiced the sin of Sodom but were flagrantly open about it (Isaiah 3:8, 9). He culminated his prophetic indictment by proclaiming, "Woe unto their soul! for they have rewarded evil unto themselves." In other words, the fall of Israel and the subsequent scattering of the ten "lost tribes" was caused by their Sodom-like sins—including homosexuality. In fact, verse 12 states, "As for my people, children are their oppressors, and women rule over them. O my people, they which lead thee cause thee to err, and destroy the way of thy paths." The Hebrew word for *women*, who ruled Israel at that time, is most interesting. Some lexicons translate it "womenlike men," or "effeminate," while others render it "men who act like women." In other words, Israel's government had been invaded by homosexuals, thus invoking the judgment of God on the nation.

Judah, the southern tribe under the leadership of King

Hezekiah and the preaching of the prophet Isaiah, turned to God and repented of their national sins; consequently, they were spared the captivity that befell the ten tribes of Israel, but less than 150 years later they again turned to the sins and corruptions of the nations surrounding them until Jerusalem was destroyed and they were led into the Babylonian captivity by King Nebuchadnezzar. In the sixteenth chapter of the prophecy of Ezekiel, he condemns Judah for being a sister to "Sodom" (vv. 46-48) and accuses them of being even worse than Sodom. Evidently, one of the rampant sins of the Hebrew people at that time, like that of Sodom before her, must have been homosexuality.

Historians are well-versed in the bisexuality of Grecian culture just three and four hundred years before Christ. Socrates was a practicing homosexual, as were most of the Greek leaders and philosophers. Plato penned an entire section in his *Symposium* exalting homosexual "love." Even Alexander the Great, often thought to be the greatest military leader of all time, had both male and female lovers. Because Greece was a small country with enormous expansionist ideas, childlessness was made illegal but homosexuality was widely accepted. The Greek warriors spent much of their lives away from home—with their lovers at their side. They felt that homosexuality helped to produce battlefield valor since they fought so fiercely to protect their lovers.

Historians verify that homosexuality was rampant in the days of Rome, particularly in the upper echelons of leadership. Sutonius, in his book *The Twelve Caesars*, indicated that fourteen out of the first fifteen emperors of Rome were homosexuals. The book chronicles the lives of these Caesars in detail, revealing their homosexual life style and demonstrating how it permeated the empire. King Nikodimes had none other than Julius Caesar as his bed partner, exulting on one occasion that he was "the queen's partner and rival in the royal bed." Caesar Augustus, it is charged, sold his services for 3000 gold pieces. He even softened the hair on his legs by burning them with a walnut shell so he would be more desirable to his lovers. Tiberius, a sadist, adopted young boys and used them cruelly. Nero seduced little boys; one, it is said, particularly met his fancy, so he had him castrated, put a bridal veil on him, and married him in an official ceremony. After the death of Nero, the next Caesar adopted the lad and continued the relationship. The baths of Caracalla in Rome were not significantly different from homosexual baths of today; you could get a bath, sex, or both. Just a few months ago, I visited the ruins of Pompeii—a Roman city of that era noted for its homosexuality. When our guide took us into a beautiful public bath which he said was "for men only," I couldn't help thinking, "Shades of New York City, San Francisco, or San Diego." No wonder both Gibbon and Toynbee concluded that homosexuality was one of the moral sins that contributed to the decline of the Roman Empire. Part of that deterioration included a population decline due to homosexuality.

Homosexuality has found its way, however secretly for fear of discovery, through many cultures and civilizations. In recent years it has been linked to such well-known personalities as "Leonardo da Vinci, Michelangelo, Christopher Marlowe, Shakespeare, Frederick the Great, Goethe, Beethoven, Tchaikovsky, Oscar Wilde, Andre Gide, Walt Whitman, W. H. Auden and Somerset Maugham—many of them considered creative geniuses."[1]

Although most historians know of its existence, they have either ignored it or treated the matter in such a casual manner as to call little attention to its existence. But with a fresh notoriety given it by such people as Hemingway and "Playwright Tennessee Williams, who acknowledges it in his *Memoirs*,"[2] gay ranks are emerging. Charles Laughton admitted it in his *Biography*, substantiated later by his wife in *Parade Magazine*.[3] During the last three decades there has been a tremendous increase in homosexuality; now some of its advocates claim there are 20 million in the United States.

Sigmund Freud's Contribution

You might rightly wonder, why this "explosion" of a problem that has been kept closeted for centuries? No single answer will suffice, but a major contributor to the present-day tendency to accept and encourage homosexuality is Dr. Sigmund Freud. Almost everyone acknowledges that he has exercised more influence on the sexual practices and standards of our day than anyone who has lived in the last one hundred years, but few people realize that also includes homosexuality.

Freud graduated from the University of Vienna in 1881 at the height of the Victorian age. In spite of his Jewish heritage, he was an atheist and very hostile to Christianity. It is widely accepted today by psychologists and others that he had many personal "hangups" that adversely influenced his theories and conclusions. A highly intelligent and insecure "mama's boy," he concluded that man's chief motivation was sexual gratification, which subconsciously drove him to nervous disorders and mental illness because it usually conflicted with religious laws and taboos. Freud's solution was to censure religious standards and principles as harmful and to urge people to give in to their repressed feelings, urges, and drives. Since he did not believe in a God who had the right to teach men what was right and wrong, he advocated "freedom of sexual expression" as an aid to mental health. Like most of his followers, Freud never did understand the human conscience that is a natural part of all human beings unless destroyed culturally or by repeated violations.

Freud's theoretical explanation for the cause of

homosexuality was really quite simple, but it caught on and spread throughout the western world. He thought that since all children are sexually curious, they are all "incestuous"—at least mentally—and that boys are particularly susceptible to their mothers (as he was). Thus a boy tends to identify with his mother rather than his father. He labeled this "the Oedipus Complex," after the Greek tragedy *Oedipus Rex*, in which Oedipus killed his father and married his mother.

The significance of Freud's contribution to the modern acceptance of homosexuality cannot be overestimated. The Victorian society of his day thought of it as a perversion against God and man and was extremely intolerant of "queens" or "fruits," as homosexuals were often called. Freud suggested it was a case of retarded psychic development in that a mother-loving boy sought a similar love from other males, so he naturally grew up to be an adult homosexual.

In other words, homosexuality was no longer to be considered an illegal form of debauchery or perversion in which one willingly engaged a person of his own sex, but a "mental illness' which one blamed on his mother. Consequently, a homosexual is not responsible for his behavior—it's his mother's fault! Removing from man the full responsibility for his behavior was a consistent pattern in Freud's theories. However, the psychiatric community officially regarded homosexuality as a form of "mental illness" until 1973.

Havelock Ellis

What Sigmund Freud was to the sexual revolution in general, Havelock Ellis was to homosexuality. A student of Freud, Ellis took vigorous issue with his teaching. Unlike Freud, "Ellis himself was possessed not only of a 'contrary sexual feeling,' but he was an enthusiast for motherhood, among

other things . . . [which] included a fervor for sexual
experimentation and a desire to understand sexual deviance.
Maybe that's why he married a female homosexual.''[4]

Although Freud's theories were being enthusiastically
embraced by the academic community, Ellis took exception
to the idea that homosexuality was a dominant mother's or a
"smother mother's" fault. Instead, he taught that it was
"inherited" and could well be a sign of greatness. In the 1930s
he revised his book, *Sexual Invasion*, and produced one of
the first explicit sex manuals.

Ellis mentioned several of the names cited earlier in this
chapter to show how many distinguished people in history
were homosexuals. He particularly listed great artists, poets,
writers, playwrights, politicians, and others. His obvious
conclusion was that they were geniuses because they were
gay. The fact that they have been great in spite of their
homosexuality didn't seem to occur to him—nor did the
possibility that they might have been greater had they been
straight.

Just four months before writing this chapter, my wife and I
visited the Sistine Chapel in Vatican City, Rome. That was
when I first became suspicious that Michelangelo might be a
homosexual. For standing there with our heads stretched back,
looking at that masterpiece of a chapel ceiling, I called Bev's
attention to the painter's obvious obsession: the male body.
In researching for this book, I discovered that
Michelangelo's homosexuality was well known among those
who wrote on the subject. Acknowledging his greatness
as a painter and sculptor, had you ever thought of the fact that
his most famous subjects were men and that he was not a
good painter of women—unless you happen to favor drawings
of muscle-bound women.

Like Freud and most others who have molded the frame-
work of modern psychological concepts, Ellis was a
committed evolutionist. Since (they say) man is an animal,

what is natural for animals is natural for man. In his book Ellis used the reports of zoologists who claimed they had observed homosexuality among the primates, leading him to conclude that it was a "natural" form of behavior. (This contradicts what I learned in discussions with curators at the San Diego Zoo, one of the world's largest, where acts of sodomy are said to be unknown among primates.) If it is a natural form of behavior and the life style of some of the world's greats, Ellis concluded that it "naturally" follows that it isn't evil or a mental illness at all, but that certain gifted people just naturally are born that way.

In order to prove his point and make homosexuality socially acceptable, Ellis selected "thirty-three male homosexuals and six lesbians . . . from the best circles of American and British scientific and intellectual communities"[5] to use as case histories. Although he admitted that his sample studies were too limited to provide any scientific conclusions, he made his conclusions anyway, which through the years have helped to lead many in the intellectual community away from Freud's view that "it's mother's fault" to the notion that "you're born with it!" No scientific evidence has ever been found to support Ellis' contention!

Fortunately for mankind, few of the "intelligentsia" are willing to accept unscientific theories without evidence, so the tragic results of Ellis' ideas were limited to the college and university, where they victimized only a small percentage of the student population and some professors. The work of popularization, however, was reserved for a now famous taxonomist. (A taxonomist is one who classifies insects and animals.)

The Kinsey Reports

The Kinsey Reports can safely be called "the Bible of the

sexual revolution." No other books by a single author have been more influential in forming the bedroom practices of the western world. I would not suggest that all of his findings are harmful, but many of us warned back in the fifties that these concepts, if given widespread distribution by the media and school system, would lead to a drastic increase in infidelity, divorce, perversion, venereal disease, and human heartache. Who can deny the accuracy of that prophecy?

Alfred Kinsey was not a trained authority on sexual behavior. "His major claim to fame was that he had spent twenty-eight years studying, classifying and writing about gallflies."[6] After publishing two volumes on that subject, he turned to human sexuality and under a grant from the Rockefeller Foundation finished a research project which formed the nucleus of *Sexual Behavior in the Human Male*, published in 1948. This book, based on two-hour interviews with 5,300 American males, offers extremely biased and in some cases dangerously erroneous information. The tragedy is that it has been quoted more than any other book of its kind by writers on the subject of sexuality during the past thirty years. Most writers who use its suggestions assume its accuracy. In 1953 his second sexual behavior manual, based on interviews with 5,940 women, purports to tell the intimate sexual practices and preferences of the "average" American woman. What Freud and Ellis did in codifying the thoughts of educators on human sexuality, Kinsey did for the general public. His books became best sellers and are almost invariably quoted as the final authority by anyone who has a bent toward sexual license to justify his behavior.

Even practicing homosexuals who may never have read his books or his report seem to know that his interviews revealed the now famous statistics that "thirty-seven percent of the male population had committed at least one homosexual act and fifty percent had responded at some time in their lives to a homosexual motivation." Kinsey said that "the ability to respond to homosexual stimuli existed in every member of the

human species."[7] He further suggested that all humans
have the capacity to respond to a person of the same sex, if
given the right circumstances and opportunity. Therefore
he concluded that the terms "heterosexual" or
"homosexual" are not adequate. Instead, everyone should
face the fact that he is potentially "bisexual."

Twentieth-century sexologists have embraced three
dominant messages. Freud taught us that any homosexual
tendencies are not our fault but that we are mentally ill, and
besides, "it's our mother's fault." Ellis instructed us that
"we're born with it, and it is a sign of greatness." Kinsey tried
to make us believe that half the people are doing it. Of the
three, Kinsey without doubt has had the most harmful effect
on the morals of America.

Summary

Can We Trust
the Kinsey Reports?

Every time I have debated sexologists on the college campus
or discussed sexuality with a member of the academic
community or their student victims, they invariably bring up
the Kinsey Reports. They refer to them authoritatively the way
I refer to the Bible. Therefore it is legitimate to ask, "Can we
really trust the Kinsey Reports?" I would like to suggest that
in spite of their prestigious influence in the western world,
they may not be scientific, scholarly, or reliable. The truth of
the matter is, they should be regarded more as propaganda
than scientific documentation. Instead of revealing accurately
the sex life of Americans, they popularize and exalt
promiscuity. For the following reasons, Kinsey Reports
should be discredited.

1. Kinsey was not objective! Everyone knows that
scientific research should be approached objectively.
However, whenever a scholar embraces a research project
with a preconceived bias, he endangers the accuracy of his

findings and certainly the reliability of his theories or conclusions. Kinsey and his researchers were sexual permissivists, though not necesssarily in their personal lives. A sexual permissivist is one who "ideally" thinks that people do not have to conform to established sexual patterns, that one's sexuality is his own business and everyone should have the right to do with his own sexuality anything he chooses. As one famous sexologist said to a group of high schoolers, pointing her finger toward heaven, "There's no one up there telling you what is right or wrong."

Most of the people identified with Kinsey researchers are not only of the sexually permissive bent (or "anything goes" crowd) but seem to maintain a decidedly anti-Christian or anti-Bible bias. One such writer, a prominent psychologist and psychotherapist, writes of the Jewish and Christian moral teachings,

> Sexual excitement *per se* was always associated with sin, even in one's sleep or one's imagination—hence, the *notion* [my emphasis] that he who looks at a woman lustfully already commits adultery in his mind. Similar attitudes continue to... reiterate our antisexual philosophy.... The later Christians proved to be even more rigorous and harsh in their antisexual edicts. Thus, broadly speaking, our mores gained their direction from Jewish history and their harshness from Christian elaborations.

He even proceeded to label our Christian moral standards "reactionary antisexual philosophy."[8] You shouldn't be surprised that a Kinsey researcher held such a view; Kinsey himself supported similar anti-Christian biases. If Kinsey's real purpose was to destroy the morals of America, we must confess that he was an extremely successful man.

2. College students are not representative! In order for a random sample to be characteristic of the American population, it should include representatives from all walks of

life. Today less than 35 percent of American young people attend college; in 1948 it was far less. And college students, who comprised the majority of Kinsey's interviewees, certainly did not then and do not now represent the other 65-70 percent of the population. College young people are notoriously more sexually permissive and curious than any other group in our society for two reasons: first, permissiveness is given the false respectability of the teaching profession, which often seems obsessed with trying to provoke young people to act like the animals they think them to be; second, college students are at the height of their greatest emotional instability (ages fifteen to twenty-four) and the peak of their sex drive. Consequently, the sexual expression of their college years is *not* typical of even the average college student's lifetime patterns and certainly not of the majority of people who never go to college. Had Kinsey's researchers interviewed construction or factory workers from ages eighteen to sixty-five, I am confident that his results would have been much different.

3. Volunteers for sex research are not typical! A person's sexual practices are still a very personal matter, and even today most people would shun discussing these intimate details with a stranger—even one in a long white coat. Thirty years ago the average person was more reluctant to reveal his sexual secrets. Consequently, what kind of people would volunteer for such a survey? I suspect it was made up of many exhibitionists, a few weirdos or kinks, and some fairly average college students—but hardly the typical American.

In short, a study of just over 10,000 college students made by humanistically oriented researchers with an anti-Judeo-Christian morality bias is hardly going to be ''representative'' of any normal group of people, particularly the ''average American male or female.'' But it did make great propaganda for anything-goes sexual permissiveness. And it has probably done more to herald the present homosexual epidemic than any other single event in the last fifty years.

Homosexual Propaganda

The propaganda barrage favoring homosexuality has increased relentlessly in newspapers, magazines, books, the schoolhouse, and even some churches. Television and films almost seem obsessed with making the American public accept homosexuality as "an alternate life style." One television network just produced a three-hour documentary on homosexuality with the effect of conveying to the public that it is natural with some people—as natural as heterosexuality is with others. Many shows and movies feature homosexuals as misunderstood, tortured, hapless victims of the cruelty imposed upon them by our Victorian morality.

As we shall see in a later chapter, the homosexual community is organized, militant, and demonstrative. As a minority movement in America it demands that we give it official sanction and acknowledge its "rights." Thousands are willing to take to the streets and proudly declare their sexual preference. They are presently challenging discriminatory practices in housing, education, and employment. What was once a secret sin, rarely mentioned, has become an epidemic sweeping the land; now it is estimated that there are five to twenty million homosexuals in America. Currently the homosexual explosion is attracting more attention than unemployment, overpopulation, or racial discrimination. What we have seen so far, however, is nothing compared to the social uproar that is coming. If you don't believe that, you haven't talked to the leaders of the homosexual movement.

CHAPTER TWO

What Is Homosexuality?

The homosexual world is quite foreign to straight people. Although they are aware it exists, their typical spirit of revulsion to homosexuality causes them to ignore it. They refer to homosexuals as "perverts," "weirdos," "queers" or worse. The current wave of propaganda makes it impossible to ignore the problem, and like most things we ignore, it certainly isn't going to go away. Consequently, it is important that straight people take the time to understand the homosexual community, which likes to refer to itself as "Gay."

One straight lady, during the height of the Dade County campaign to reestablish the laws allowing homosexual job discrimination, said, "I don't understand why Anita Bryant is getting so uptight about homosexuality. I'd rather have my daughter taught by a homosexual than by some male who might try to rape her." That mother revealed her utter ignorance of homosexuality. She was thinking only of a sexual experience—not the much more important conditioning process that a homosexual teacher would be inclined to follow hour after hour, day after day, until her daughter was taught to think favorably about homosexuality.

Homosexuality is not just a sexual experience; it is a total life style. Homosexuals think differently than straights, they act differently, and as individuals they experience sex differently. We shall see that their drive is not related to the glands, genes, or hormones, but is a learned behavior that usually starts early in life and, more than almost any other practice, affects the individual's total life and thinking process. The homosexual world and the straight world are polar opposites. Until you have seen two men dancing together or two lesbians openly kissing each other on the mouth, two men affectionately embracing or a man dressed up like a woman, including false eyelashes, rouge, and lipstick, you aren't prepared to believe that the homosexual world is a different life than anything you are familiar with. Such sights usually turn "straights" off so quickly that they look no further.

Although I have counseled many homosexual men and women through the years and spent hours trying to help them, I did not feel I could write this book until I had observed homosexual life as it really is. Most of my experience was with individuals who wanted help or with young people whose parents had brought them to me for counseling. I had seen the usual "gay couples"—two men or two women with matching outfits, wearing wedding rings and holding hands in public— but I had never witnessed their "haunts," the places they go to pick up partners or put on entertainment. So I visited some of the places they frequent; I've seen them in action, and I can assure you—it's a different world!

Like most subcultures, the homosexual community has its own vocabulary. They understand ours, of course, but we don't always understand theirs. They have attached definitions to certain words and terms that give them a whole new meaning. To help you understand them, consider some of their most commonly used expressions.

Definitions

Homosexual:

A man or woman who engages in sexual activity with another member of the same sex. Such activity usually leads to an orgasmic experience.

Lesbian:

A woman homosexual. She usually brings her female partner to sexual climax by manipulation of the clitoris with either her finger or tongue.

Latent Homosexual:

A cruel and harmful term (attributed to Sigmund Freud) suggesting that some people are born with homosexual tendencies. Many people believe that men who use effeminate gestures and mannerisms or women who act masculine possess "latent homosexual tendencies." This is a lie. Studies show that over 80 percent of the "effeminate" acting men and masculine women are heterosexual.

Pseudosexual:

A person who possesses certain superficial characteristics that cause people to erroneously label them gay when in reality they are not.

Heterosexual:

Those who confine their sexual activity to members of the opposite sex

Bisexual:

One who has sexual relations with both sexes.

Transvestite:	A person who likes to wear one or more pieces of clothing of the opposite sex. Contrary to popular opinion, most of these people remain heterosexual, marry, and raise a family (if the spouse can overlook this idiosyncrasy).
Straight:	A heterosexual person.
Gay:	Favorite term of the homosexual community to describe themselves.
Closet Gay:	A homosexual who, for personal or professional reasons, hides or covers his homosexuality.
Queen:	An effeminate male homosexual (also called "nelly" or "fairy").
Closet Queen:	An effeminate man who practices homosexual acts when he can but who keeps his practice a closely guarded secret for personal reasons.
Old Queen:	An old, effeminate homosexual male, usually no longer desirable as a sex partner, who often experiences extreme loneliness and has the highest unhappiness quotient and suicide rate.
Drag:	Female clothes used by a male to impersonate a female.
Drag Queen:	A queen dressed in drag on the prowl.
Faggot:	The stereotyped homosexual; a limp-wristed, feminine acting homosexual often looked down upon by other gays.
Butch:	A masculine or super-masculine

	homosexual. Many wear boots. leather clothing, or extremely tight-fitting clothing that show off their muscles and emphasize their genitalia.
Trouble:	Butch that may cause trouble
Sadist and Masochist, or ''Slave Master'':	One who adds brutality or cruelty to sexuality. Some punish their partners; others prefer to be punished or tortured themselves.
Sodomy:	Anal intercourse between males.
Fellatio:	Oral copulation when one homosexual puts his penis in the other's mouth, where it is sucked until orgasm occurs.
Cruise:	A sexually stimulated gay out looking for a partner.
Gay Bars:	The places in which gays congregate for dancing, pickups, and sexual contacts.
Baths:	Special baths frequented by gays when looking for sex. Gang sex often occurs in such places.
Hustler:	A male prostitute.
Chicken:	A young homosexual.
Chicken Hawk:	An older homosexual who seeks to pick up a ''chicken.''

Beware of Stereotypes

Homosexuals get extremely ''testy'' about the straight person's tendency to put him into a neat little stereotyped

package. After looking beneath the surface more thoroughly,
I can understand their irritation; homosexuals are individuals
who come in as many variegated forms (and are as different)
as heterosexuals. A most interesting interview with a
homosexual in preparation for this book brought that to light
graphically. During our three-hour talk, the former police
sergeant with an impeccable ten-year record with the San
Diego Police Department referred three times to the fact that
he detested the "limp-wristed faggots who act like women."
He was a masculine gentleman who preferred the company
of men like himself. Very honestly, I was surprised, but
further research disclosed that my friend was not an exception.
For instance, David Kopay, former professional football
player for the Washington Redskins, shocked the sports world
with his book, *The David Kopay Story*, in which he "came
out" and revealed his homosexuality. Since then some big
names in the National and American football conferences
have been suspected of being homosexuals, though few have
been willing to make it as public as did Kopay.

Now that we acknowledge that no set stereotype can be
admitted for homosexuals, let me suggest at least four basic
types that exist.

One. The "Faggot Queen"

Seventy-five percent or more of the straight community immediately think of this type of person when "homosexuality" is mentioned.
The faggot queen openly flaunts his homosexuality, actually
cultivates female gestures and body movements, and wears
feminine clothing. An associate of mine regularly frequented
a hair dresser named George whose extremely feminine
mannerisms annoyed her, yet she regularly returned to his
shop because of his excellent work. One day George was
replaced by a "woman" look-alike, heavily made up, who
spoke with a voice obviously cultivated to sound feminine.

"From now on, I want you to call me Georgette," he said.
Some straights can handle that kind of switch; my friend
could not.

I had a similar experience when I received a distress call
from the chaplain at the city jail. A prisoner had asked that
I call on him right away. Even if I had recognized his name,
I would not have been prepared for the man dressed up like a
woman who greeted me through the glass divider in the jail
visiting booth. His handsome features were adorned with
lipstick, rouge, plucked eyebrows, and false eyelashes. A
number of prisoners have asked me to use my pastoral
influence to get them out of jail, but he was the first one who
said, "If you don't get me out of here right away, these men
will kill me; I've already been raped three times." This
young man was working hard at being a "drag queen." Such
men usually like to be pursued by homosexuals, and although
they may do anything their sex partner requires, they usually
prefer to remain passive and receive anal intercourse.

Two. The "Closet Queen"

Far more numerous than faggot
queens are closet queens. Their
sexual preferences are usually
similar to their more exhibitionist
counterparts, but they live a double life. At work or at home
they keep their homosexuality a well-guarded secret, but
socially they may put on "drag" or female attire in pursuit of
sexual contacts. More frequently they just act more feminine
than masculine all the time and enjoy being picked up by a
"butch" type when they go out cruising. They may be found
in almost every conceivable profession. No matter how
straight you are, you have probably met many, were served
faithfully by them, and may not have had any reason to
suspect that they were homosexuals. On the other hand, you
may have met *graceful* men you suspected of being
homosexuals, but who in truth were not. That is one reason

you should be extremely careful not to judge people. Most men who have a sensitive nature, were raised without benefit of an adequate male image in the home, may not have been athletically inclined, and were attracted to the more "cerebral" fields, are every bit as manly as any of the more "masculine" types. The same is true of a lesbian; you cannot tell by mannerisms or appearances whether she is sexually a woman or a man. Homosexuals themselves can tell, if the person wants to be provocative. They have a hidden language and means of communication unknown by straights.

In short, never put the "fairy" or "queen" tag on anyone unless you have abundant evidence; then, if it concerns you, go to that person privately. Many people, particularly the young, have been harmfully affected by false accusations.

Three. "The Butch" or the "Macho Butch"

This homosexual may be extremely masculine in his mannerisms, or he may try to be. He often wears leather jackets, open, tight-fitting shirts, and skin-tight jeans that call attention to bulging genitals; he may have an obsession with physical fitness, weight lifting, and bulging biceps. His intense ego drives him to the gymnasium, where for hours he artificially pumps up his muscles to gain him looks of adulation from other males as he wends his way through the homosexual haunts dressed in skin-tight attire. In extreme cases his fondest dreams make him the object of attention wherever he goes, and he fantasizes that every other male craves his body.

The sexual preferences of the swaggering "butch" are usually aggressive, but it is not uncommon for him to be attracted to another "butch" and in the height of sexual passion take turns being the "passive" or "initiator." Some, however, are "phony butch" types who act like tough guys in the bar but prefer being the passive partner in the bedroom.

"Butch" homosexuals are more likely to get into sadomasochism than queens, who tend to be more gentle by nature.

Like the "queens," "butch" homos may lead a double life or they may flaunt their sexual preference. Those who pursue a double life usually have two wardrobes, consisting of their work outfits and their homosexual duds. A professional man may be a "clothesaholic" and sport the very latest styles, featuring the finest tailoring—by day. At night you wouldn't believe he was the same person.

Consider the handsome, athletic, forty-year-old single attorney who wears three-piece suits by day and "leathers" by night. His law partners, who "hate homosexuals," aren't even suspicious of his sexual preference, even though he has good rapport with homosexuals, who direct all their legal business to him. Because he spends every lunch hour at the gymnasium working out, is extremely masculine, and is openly admired by the secretaries in the office, his associates consider him "normal." They don't know that the woman he escorts to the office parties or social events is a lesbian friend who serves as his "business cover" or that he does the same for her as she attempts to maintain a heterosexual "front." But away from the office he cares nothing for women—just men. This story is true and could be reproduced in almost every legitimate profession, including the crafts and construction fields.

Four. The "Typical Homosexual"

Yes, in spite of the homosexual's outcry to the contrary, there is a "typical homosexual," though neither a queen nor a butch. To all outside appearances he is just like the "typical hetero"—Mr. Joe Average. He doesn't seem any more feminine or masculine than the average person in the light of his background, temperament, and vocation. When this person "comes out" or reveals his sexual preference, most of his friends are surprised and some refuse to believe it, saying, "He seemed so normal." This type of homosexual makes up the majority of homosexuals, and it is this group that is really growing. The reason Mr. Average Homosexual appears more normal than the others is quite simple: most human beings are just average people, and homosexuals are people! They may be "different" in their sexual preferences from 90 to 95 percent of the rest of the population, but most of them dress the same as straights, act like straights, obey the laws of the land to the same degree, bleed when cut, and are stung inwardly when offended. Until straights accept these facts, they will neither understand homosexuals nor be able to help them.

Homosexual Promiscuity

Since the homosexual's preference sets him apart from the heterosexual majority, not his everyday dress or other activities, it is important that we consider his sexual conduct. Three significant factors emerge.

**One.
Same Sex
Preference** The best known characteristic of homosexuals is that they prefer to have sexual relations with members of their own sex rather than the opposite sex. In spite of the fact that this tendency represents only about 4 to 6 percent of the population, many sociologists insist, as do the homosexuals themselves, that it is perfectly normal. Opposite sexual attraction has always been considered "normal" and is still the norm for 95 percent or more of the population. The fact that homosexuals represent such a small minority of the population should be ample proof that it is *not* normal unless by some trick of mental logic you

can make it perfectly ordinary to have 95 percent of the people
function sexually one way and 5 percent or so another. The
danger in that kind of logic is that you accept homosexuality
as "inevitable" instead of seeking a cause or logical
explanation, such as "learned behavior." If the imprecise use
of statistics seems confusing, it is because no one *really* knows
how many homosexuals there are. Kinsey said 4 percent, Troy
Perry claims 6 percent, and the militants want us to believe it
is as high as 20 million; 4 or 5 percent or eight to ten million
is probably closer to the truth, and many of those would like to
"come out" of it.

Two. Sexual Promiscuity

Moral fidelity among homosexuals
is almost unknown. Even those who
enter into a lifetime love relationship
with another usually play the field
frequently. One psychologist writer suggests that it is not
uncommon for a homosexual to "have sex" with as many as
2,000 different people in a lifetime. Even if he is only half
right in his estimate, such promiscuity taxes the imagination
of even the most immoral heterosexual. During the past
twenty-five years that I have been counseling people, I have
interviewed many sexually promiscuous individuals, but none
even came close to that number of different "affairs." One
woman suffering from orgasmic malfunction held the record
for my studies; she claimed to have had relations "with
almost one hundred men" in her lifetime. Frankly, I thought
she was exaggerating.

Contrast that record for heterosexual infidelity with the
estimate of 2,000 sexual partners (not only by the above
mentioned psychologist but also by several homosexuals I
have talked to) and you begin to see the enormous difference
in the sexual life style of the homo and the hetero.

Homosexuals don't start out to be that promiscuous, but
are usually drawn into it because of a love relationship with a

person they admire. When this person moves on to his next partner, the first is left with an intense feeling of emptiness that soon gives way to a quest for another partner, and before long he becomes as promiscuous as others. Anyone requiring loyalty, fidelity, and oneness is doomed to disappointment in the homosexual life style.

Three. Sex for Its Own Sake

The sex drive was created in man by God for both propagation and pleasure, but because of its very personal nature, requiring the baring of those intimate parts of the body we normally shield from the eyes of other people, it is to be confined to one person with whom we share our total self. Just as you naturally keep certain secrets from the general public and reveal them only to someone you love and can trust, so by instinct man shields his sexual expression from others until he finds that person he grows to love and trust and with whom he can share his entire being—including his private sex organs. Ideally, sexual intercourse should be an expression of love.

Sex is not love! Animals have sex and most by nature are promiscuous. Men are not animals (though many learn to act that way), but when they reduce sex to the same level as animal sexuality, it becomes sex for sex's sake—not love. Whether in a heterosexual or a homosexual relationship, sex without love is an inadequate human experience! In our book *The Act of Marriage*, subtitled *The Beauty of Sexual Love*, my wife and I tried to show that sex in marriage should be the culmination of love. The couple whose sexual orgasms are the climax of many intimate expressions of love, including their mental, emotional, and physical contacts, enjoys a oneness that easily withstands other personal temptations and becomes the most satisfying of all human experiences.

Homosexuals (and, unfortunately, many heterosexuals who succumb to promiscuity) never experience that soul-satisfying oneness with another human being which says, ''I love you so much that I saved myself from all others and give myself exclusively to you so that together we may experience the sublime expression of our love—mutual sexual orgasm.'' Instead, a sexual appetite is built up until the priority in life becomes the sexual experience. Although it is biologically satisfying for a time, it becomes a parade of nameless faces and empty people with whom the homosexual shares little except his body. The older he becomes, the less satisfying does he find sex for its own sake.

Four. An Insatiable Quest for the Erotic

Although the homosexual community does not discuss this aspect of their sex life freely with straight people, the known practices of the homosexual clearly indicate that his sex drive is rarely satisfied. But whether homosexual or heterosexual, sex for its own sake will always lead to a quest for ''more, more, more!'' The man who truly loves his wife may enjoy experimentation occasionally, but surveys suggest that together they usually settle for two or three favorite positions or techniques and use them most of their lives. Those who engage in sex for sex's sake (married or otherwise) invariably want to experiment with and study every conceivable approach, gimmick, or position, and they are never satisfied. That is even more true of homosexuals than heterosexuals, probably because two men are often given to demanding greater degrees of experimentation than a man and woman. The homosexual's quest for the erotic reveals itself in many ways. My interviews showed that most homosexuals start out with oral stimulation of the penis and graduate to anal penetration. Many who are active sodomites today confessed that they were ''repulsed'' by their first encounter. Gradually, as they discovered that the anus has nerve endings which respond to stimuli just as does the glans penis or a woman's clitoris, they built up an appetite for it and craved not only sodomy but any new thing that would excite, stimulate, and bring an orgasm.

One doctor, an acknowledge homosexual, pointed to an increase in hospital emergency rooms of cases of "rectal abscesses and infections of the intestines." He further stated that "damage to the wall of the intestine can lead to peritonitis, which can develop into a life-and-death-situation, as can a ripped colon. We're seeing a lot of that now, too." Upon questioning, he indicated that this increase was caused by homosexuals forcing objects of larger and larger size into each other's anal canal. Doctors have removed "whiskey glasses, bananas, coke bottles" and almost "anything that will fit." A doctor told me recently that while serving in a hospital emergency room he was flabbergasted to discover a large stone imbedded in one man's rectum so deeply that it had to be removed surgically. Another surgeon told me he has had to remove warts from the anuses of many homosexuals. "Such surgical need is a dead giveaway of their sex style," he said. One doctor noted, "A person skilled at receiving fists (which is a current fad) has already damaged his sphincter muscle . . . which leads to anal incompetence . . . dribbling or leaking of the stool." Another doctor, deeply concerned about the homosexual community because he was one himself, said, "There's a near epidemic of syphilis and gonorrhea—in the throat," and he went on to point out that most homosexuals don't realize that the throat is as vulnerable to venereal disease as the rectum.

Such bizarre extremes are naturally the result of an inordinate quest for "more, more, more." What else could lead homosexuals to what they call "gang bangs," where a group of them will enter into an uninhibited orgy to see how many orgasms they can experience—and give—in a single day. One former homosexual (now an active Christian)

claimed that as a young man he had as many as nine
ejaculations in a single day. As incredible as it may seem, he
was not the only one I interviewed who made such a claim.
It is impossible for a straight person to imagine the
preoccupation with sex that obsesses many young
homosexuals. In fact, they are regularly disinterested in
gainful employment—their interest is sex, not work. Besides,
when a man overindulges his sex glands, he doesn't have
much energy left for work.

One of the alarming practices that comes out of this
insatiable quest for the erotic is sadomasochism. In recent
years doctors have reported an increase of patients who
obviously have been brutalized during sex practices, in some
cases resulting in murder or accidental death. You might
wonder how a man could possibly develop into a violent
sadist. The answer is "very gradually." In his quest for more,
more, and more erotic sex, the man with a cruel or sadistic
disposition begins to experiment with pain-inflicting objects
from needles and pins to chairs and icepicks. Only the
imagination restricts the expression of a homosexual's
"sexual preference."

Most of the well-intentioned heterosexuals who campaign
for more recognition and understanding of the homosexuals
have no comprehension of what really goes on in a gay orgy,
nor do they realistically face the fact that most homosexuals
live that way at some time in their lives. The so-called "love
relationship" that exists between two men is not the usual
homosexual life style. It is true that as they get older,
homosexuals tend to seek out a lasting relationship with
another who shares their same sex preference. Some may
even enjoy lengthy relationships of eighteen to twenty-two
years' duration, and I have heard of some that lasted even
longer. But for most, homosexuality provides only a series of
short, meaningless, or hurtful experiences that prepare them

for the "gay bars," "the baths," the local "fire island,"
where anything goes. Much of a homosexual's life is spent
"cruising" in the attempt to make contact with another
person. More often than not, his search leads to a hurried
sexual encounter with an unknown partner he would not even
recognize the next day if he passed him on the street. That
may be sex—but it certainly isn't love!

Gay
It
Isn't!

Hollywood was shocked at the news
that a handsome forty-seven-year-old film star at the peak of
his career committed suicide. Idolized by women around the
world, he possessed everything a man could ask—except
happiness. Recently an investigative reporter had penned his
biography, disclosing to the general public what Hollywood
insiders have known for years: "Mr. Everything" was
homosexual. The new book reveals that he was anything but
happy. Experiencing a succession of male lovers who could
not give themselves to him exclusively, he went from one
wretched emotional trauma to another over a period of years
until he ended it all.

Not many years ago the greatest sex symbol in recent
Hollywood history died of an overdose of sleeping potion. For
years men threw themselves at her feet and several had
proposed marriage, some of which she accepted. But after her
death, it was revealed that she had been involved with lesbians,
which could account for her desperate unhappiness just prior
to the time of her death.

Do these tragic illustrations of homosexuals' unhappiness
sound extreme? Don't count on it. Every counselor that I have
interviewed acknowledged that homosexuals are

unquestionably more miserable than straight people. The same was indicated in the case histories I read as well as in my own counseling interviews. Let me tell you about the nicest homosexual I ever knew.

Toby was an executive for a large corporation in our city, a very good man in every way that I could see, and a regular member of our church. He was active in the singles group and much sought after by the fair sex, whom he dated occasionally. I noticed he was always very discreet with them and never seemed to get involved for more than a short time, but I never gave his sexual preference a second thought. One day he introduced me to a seven-year-old boy who he said was a relative's child that he was trying to adopt and raise. About that time, Sally the school teacher entered the group, and it wasn't long before they wanted to get married. "I've always wanted to be the mother of a son," she said. "Toby and I are great friends, have so much in common, and are so much in love that we think we will be very happy together." I wished them God's blessing, and they were married.

I will never forget the tragic day Sally came weeping into my office, perhaps three months after their wedding. "It's all over! Toby has left me. He quit his job, took his son, and moved away." Then she explained, "Toby is a homosexual. We could never sexually consummate our marriage." My heart literally ached as she described the agony she and her mate had passed through. Evidently he wanted desperately to make a go of it with Sally, but couldn't. He was very loving and tender to her until she started to undress for bed. Then he broke out in nervous perspiration and was so obviously miserable that she didn't argue when he said he had to get out of the house and go for a walk. Every night for weeks he made some excuse to stay up late or be "too tired"—anything to avoid lovemaking. Finally he broke down and wept like a baby, sobbing out the agonizing confession: "Sally, I'm homosexual! As much as I love you, I cannot function as a husband.'' With that he walked out of all our lives. If that is "gay," who needs it?

Sally was more fortunate than some women I've counseled, for their men were not gentle or manly enough to take the blame upon themselves. Instead, they turned angrily on their brides, subjecting them either to emotional or physical torture, or both. Many women were seriously shaken psychologically, positive they were no longer appealing to men.

Twelve days after the wedding, an attractive forty-eight-year-old widow I had married to a fifty-year-old university music professor sent for me from a local psychiatric ward. She had come unglued when her culture-loving and gracious gentleman friend with whom she "had so many things in common" turned out to be a homosexual. She certainly didn't consider his homosexual life style so "gay," and in fairness to him, he didn't either.

Why Pick on "Gay"?

Not many years ago "gay" meant "fun" and was a word utilized by all kinds of people. As far as I can discover, the term "gay blade" was first used in England during the seventeenth century to describe what we refer to as a "swinger" today—the Don Juan type or ladies' man who seemed to live a gay life. (Actually, many such lotharios died a painful death of syphilis.) But "gay" was strictly a heterosexual word. Historian Arthur M. Schlesinger, Jr., objects to this synonym for homosexuality by saying, "Gay used to be one of the most agreeable words in the language. Its appropriation by a notably morose group is an act of piracy."[9] In recent years the homosexual crowd has taken over the word until the rest of us are reluctant to use it. Now we continually hear about "gay rights," "gay pride," "gay parade," "gay bars and baths," and "gay life style."

I'm aware that all gays aren't miserable all the time. From interviews with them and some of the case histories I have studied, I readily acknowledge that many of them feel happiness at times and in their own way experience moments of ecstasy. But I prefer not to use their favorite word to describe themselves because it is deceitful. "Gay" isn't gay for the majority of homosexuals, not even some of the time. It is more of a propaganda word than a definition, an illusion to hide the loneliness their way of life imposes upon them. If as much as 6 percent of our population is homosexual, then homosexuals face a suicide rate several times higher than that of the straight community. One writer claims that 50 percent of the suicides in America can be attributed to homosexuality. In my book *How to Win Over Depression*, I reported that the minimum number of estimated suicides in America runs between 50,000 and 70,000 annually. If that writer is right, from 25,000 to 35,000 homosexuals commit suicide each year in the greatest country on earth. If these statistics are valid, then the suicide rate among the homosexual community is twelve to fourteen times greater than that of the straight community.

In a *San Francisco Chronicle* story in March of 1976, the operator of a large venereal disease clinic with an annual budget of over one million dollars a year reported that 70 percent of their clients were homosexuals (San Francisco is often referred to as "the homosexual capital of the world," with more "gay bars" and homosexual haunts per capita than any other major city). One homosexual newspaper lavishly praised a Los Angeles clinic that handles 7,500 VD patients a month. It costs the taxpayers of California approximately $20 million a year to treat homosexuals for VD. Taking massive doses of penicillin to cure VD certainly is not gay!

Joe Ledbetter, a former homosexual, admits that "he and many other homosexuals lived on S.S.I., or tax money, paid each month to the homosexuals because they were suicidal and nonemployable, or for similar reasons. Ledbetter received $259 per month in tax-free money from the government. He had been receiving similar payments for more than four years at the time of his interview.''[10] Since when does a lifetime of welfarism ever result in happiness? For short-time emergency rations welfare is a lifesaver. But when it becomes a way of life, it strips the recipient of the self-respect and expectation of productivity that every human being needs for happiness.

In his book *Eros Defiled*, Dr. John White, who acknowledges he was a reluctant homosexual participant in his youth, says, ''Homosexuals, by and large, are unhappy people. They are unhappy because however successful their fight against discrimination may be, they will never gain either understanding or acceptance by the straight world. They are also unhappy because they suffer a more than average share of loneliness and rejection—even at times by their gay friends.''[11]

Leaders of the gay liberation movement use every modern means at their disposal to flood the minds of today's youth with the notion that homosexuality is a ''gay'' life style. At the time when many youth seem angry by nature at the ''establishment,'' the gay libbers try to convince them that the establishment is ''straight.'' Consequently, straight becomes the enemy and the ''gay'' life is transformed into ''the good life.'' To help counteract this devious concept, I want to present sixteen reasons why ''gay'' isn't gay. Hopefully you can use some of these reasons to enable young people who may be sexually ambivalent for a time in their life to see the homosexual life for what it really is before they become enslaved.

One. Loneliness

Everyone is lonely at some time in his life—that is perfectly natural— but homosexuals experience an enormous amount of loneliness, far more than the average straight person. And be sure of this: lonely people are not happy!

Murray Norris, a reporter who has studied the California homosexual scene, states,

> One of the biggest problems with homosexuals is their own loneliness. In homosexuals' own publications, in the writings of psychiatrists who treat them, in the words of the ministers who try to help them, there is this constant repetition of the loneliness of the homosexual life. This loneliness has led many homosexuals into drugs and alcoholism. One psychologist may have gone only a bit far when he says, "Not every alcoholic is a homosexual, but every homosexual is an alcoholic."
>
> Dr. Melvin Anchell, medical doctor and practicing psychiatrist, points out that homosexuals are seldom satisfied with their relationships and are constantly seeking new thrills, or new forms of sexuality. They head into sado-masochism. They are frequently vicious with their own partners and with others.
>
> Whoever decided to call homosexuals "gay" must have had a terrible sense of humor.[12]

A practicing "gay," who wants to remain anonymous, said of homosexuals, "They have a wonderful compensatory mechanism that allows them to act 'up' even when they feel down. The word 'gay' says it all. The most unhappy gay learns to put on a gay face. It is almost a religion among gays to be 'up,' to live."

No wonder young people are deceived with the idea that homosexuality is "gay."

I don't wish to belabor the point, but it is extremely important that all prospective homosexuals and those who are seeking to work with them recognize that one of the big lie techniques of the "Gay Lib" movement is to present their life

style as "gay." The young often mistake the apparent aura of
love in "gay haunts" as a true, caring love. It is anything but
that. The uninitiated should beware; it is a thinly disguised lust
that seeks to gain a sexual partner, even if it means stealing
him from someone else. After the "love affair" runs its course,
the youthful homosexual is dumped and loneliness sets in.
After such times of rejection, experienced by all homosexuals
sooner or later (and with most it is a majority of the time), the
intense loneliness that sets in all too often leads to suicide. It
would be better to call the gay life a "get" life, for in actuality
"gay" gets another victim and leads him into loneliness.

Two. Incredible Promiscuity

One of the primary forces in sexual
motivation is often the basic desire to
share one's intimate self with "an
intimate other." The very nature of
the relationship requires fidelity to produce lasting happiness.
As a marriage counselor for years, I have noticed that the most
devastating experience in marriage is infidelity. No marriage
that is plagued by unfaithfulness will last. The same
psychological need for faithfulness exists between
homosexuals, but only a few experience it, for, as we have
already seen, most homosexuals live with promiscuity.
Almost all counselors agree that lesbians tend to effect much
longer relationships than homosexual men. This may be due
to the feminine tendency to desire more stable relationships,
their lower sex drive, and greater reluctance toward
uninhibited sexual experimentation. This, of course, depends
on the individual.

One thing is certain: anyone desiring a long-term intimate
love relationship is much less likely to find it in homosexuality
than in the heterosexual world. And the frequency of
alienation of affection, jealousy, heartache, and all that goes
with the trauma of breaking off a close relationship is much
more apt to be part of the life style of the homosexual.

Three.
Deceit

Only two options are open to homosexuals. They can "come out," announce their homosexuality to the world, and face the rejection and ridicule that many in the straight community still subject them to, or they can hide it, which is the way all homosexuals begin and which remains the life style of the majority. Anyone in the closet about his homosexuality must learn deceit to keep his closet door closed.

After my initial homosexual counseling experience a number of years ago, I called a psychologist friend for advice. He surprised me by warning, "I have found in dealing with homosexuals that they will lie, cheat, steal, and do almost anything to keep their secret hidden." Through the years as I have counseled other homosexuals, I have often considered his advice, for I have never met an exception. In fact, most homosexuals are the best liars you will ever meet. Their techniques of distortion or evasion are almost impeccable. They have learned the art of deception so well that they can look you straight in the eye and tell a barefaced lie while maintaining a look of complete innocence. Many times they have outmaneuvered me. One wife exclaimed, "My husband is such a convincing liar that he can almost make me believe what he says, even though I was present and know things didn't happen as he said."

Liars cannot be lastingly happy. Sooner or later a web of lies will entrap them. That's why so many homosexuals constantly fear that their life of deceit will bring them to that awful moment of truth when someone they love looks them in the eye and asks, "Are you homosexual?" As President Lincoln said, "You can fool some of the people all of the time, and all of the people some of the time, but you can't fool all of the people all of the time."

Deceit inevitably generates inner misery because of the insecurity and fear that mounts every time a liar discusses something with a friend. Since many of the questions he answers and statements he makes are untrue, during each conversation his mind races in a vain attempt to remember what he said the last time they discussed the matter. Even if he tells the same lie the second time, he has no assurance that he told the same one before, which produces acute mental tension due to insecurity and fear. Truth is basic, which is why the man who tells the truth always enjoys a sound mind. Each time he deals with a subject, he tells the same story. One of the reasons a homosexual subconsciously withdraws from people is that he fears that his fabrications will catch up with him. However, such isolation only compounds his loneliness. This deceit also explains why he enjoys the company of his homosexual friends. He doesn't have to be on his guard so much around them; they know his true life style. Around them he can relax.

Four.
Guilt

A new and very popular book on homosexuality recounts actual interviews with seventeen different homosexuals from all walks of life. Most of these accounts describe how they first became involved (often in lurid detail). I noticed this in all the interviews: their first few encounters caused them to be guilt-ridden. Some learned to overcome their guilt, but several never did. A natural stigma of shame and guilt seems to be attached to homosexuality. The psychological community tries to blame that on our culture or religion, but it is so basic and consistent that we must find a better explanation: it is intuitive. Of one thing you can be certain—guilt always produces misery, and homosexuals experience such guilt-producing misery more than straights.

Five.
Alienation
from God

Every man possesses a capacity for God which, if satisfied, brings its own sense of fulfillment. Without that fulfillment, a sense of emptiness grows inwardly. Guilt alienates a person from God and leaves his capacity for God (which Pascal called our "God-shaped vacuum") continually empty. This alienation from God, together with a similar estrangement from loved ones, is often more than he can bear. Generally speaking, homosexuals look sadder and experience more depression and loneliness than other people. This emptiness and lack of inner communion with God is one of the major causes of the high degree of alcoholism, drug addiction, and suicide that many counselors believe exists among homosexuals. Guilt left unattended ultimately takes one of three courses:

First, it makes the person so miserable that he will call upon God for mercy. If properly introduced to the sacrifice of Jesus Christ for his sins, he may invoke the name of the Lord for forgiveness and salvation. This is the major purpose of our conscience in the first place—to bring us to God.

Second, he may try to live under the tyranny of guilt, becoming more and more miserable until he cracks up emotionally or commits suicide.

The third alternative is that after continually violating his conscience by repeated homosexual acts, he sears his conscience "as with a hot iron." No human being is born conscienceless, but sensitivity to evil can be erased—witness some of the hardened criminals on death row who freely admit that they would just as soon kill a man as look at him. Such abnormality, void of compassion, cannot be comprehended by most people. The homosexual doesn't start out that way, but by constantly violating his conscience, he renders it inoperative. A conscienceless person may be reasonably happy during the first half of his life, but later his alienation from God becomes an increased cause of loneliness.

Six.
Strong Tendency
toward
Selfishness

A Chicago psychiatrist reports, "The two most selfish clients I deal with are the alcoholic and the homosexual. Of the two I think homosexuals are prone to be the

more selfish.'' Certainly I have found it so with those with
whom I have counseled, and other counselors agree. When
one takes into account all the heartache and suffering
homosexuals cause other innocent people, particularly those
who love them most, it becomes quite clear that homosexuals
are usually very selfish people. Of course, whether
heterosexual or homosexual, selfish individuals are never
happy.

Homosexual case studies reveal a heavy use of the personal
pronoun and an adamant demanding of their own way and
rights. One frankly admitted, ''When it comes to my sexual
needs, it should begin and end with what I think of me . . .
what I want for me.'' Another freely acknowledged, ''There
are many advantages to being homosexual. *You are
responsible solely for yourself*. If you earn a decent living, you
can live quite well; if you earn a mere existence, you can still
live as opposed to surviving, which would be the case if one
were married. The homosexual life is freer. The homosexual
is more independent, and independence is the most attractive
aspect of homosexuality. Is that selfish? Perhaps, but I think
we have reached a point in time where many people can
choose to live 'selfishly' rather than by the old and expected
norm of 'sharing' your life with a family. I do not wish to be
a breadwinner. Furthermore, *I do not like to have people
hanging on me: I am dependent on no one and I do not wish for
anyone to be dependent on me*.'' (Emphasis added by author)
These actual testimonies from hard-core homosexuals are not
exceptions; they are all but universal. The speakers do not
understand that a selfish philosophy of life ultimately leads
to an unhappy life. In addition, it violates many divine
principles, such as ''Give and it shall be given unto you'' or
''Do unto others as you would have them do unto you.'' It
produces misery because ''Whatsoever a man soweth, that
shall he also reap.''

I do not wish to imply that heterosexuals are not also
selfish, for self-indulgence is the supreme cause of divorce

and the breakdown of family life today. My point is that homosexuals are almost universally selfish people whose preoccupation with self has helped to produce their life style. How can they hope to gain lasting happiness?

**Seven.
Rejection**

Only a heart of stone, impervious to the heartaches of others, would be unmoved by the unhappiness homosexuals experience through rejection. It is natural for every human being to desire the love and acceptance of his family, peer group, friends, and other associates. All psychologists agree that love and acceptance are basic human needs, and a person's happiness is largely dependent on an adequate supply of those needs. But of all types of people in society today, the minority that feels the most rejected and consequently the most unhappy is the homosexual community.

Fear of rejection is often uppermost in the mind of a homosexual after his first sexploit, and parental rejection is almost universal today (TV brainwashing notwithstanding). Straight parents are usually crushed, disappointed, frustrated, and confused when they discover their child is homosexual. In my opinion, nothing is more devastating and heartbreaking than the rejection of one's parents. If you think that is an exaggerated statement, it only proves that you have never listened to rejected counselees weep the heartaches that originate in childhood rejection. Some never regain any semblance of self-image, even when later in life the parents apologize and try to accept them. Parental rejection leaves psychic scars that only the grace of God can remove, and even then it takes time.

The homosexual is subject not only to parental rejection but to repudiation by most of the straight population, including friends, business associates, neighbors, authorities, and the general public. But what most homosexuals do not realize is that they are extremely vulnerable to rejection by fellow homosexuals, particularly by men who, as we have seen, are prone to be promiscuous. Almost all homosexuals can tell of several heart-rending experiences when a "lover" cast them aside for another. After such rejections many homosexual suicides occur. Admittedly, heterosexuals go through lover rejections too, but not nearly as often as homosexuals do. Anyone considering homosexuality as a life style ought to face the realistic fact that it is extremely conducive to rejection.

Eight. Difficulty of Maintaining Lasting Relationships

Most people desire a lasting love relationship in which they can share their total intimate self with another. The very nature of men makes it more precarious for two men to try to establish and maintain such a relationship than for two persons of opposite sex. One homosexual demonstrated great insight into this problem when he stated, "It is more difficult for homosexuals to have ongoing relationships because there are still no ground rules. We have no marriage certificates or social sanctions to bind us. No children hold us together—which is both a plus and a minus. It takes a tremendous amount of learning for two men to live together successfully—much more so than a man and a woman as all men are trained from birth to be the breadwinner and the dominant factor in their homes. Thus, conflict can arise between two males who are lovers. It takes a great deal of winding down of roles for a relationship between two men to work."[13]

It has already been acknowledged that some homosexuals do indeed develop and maintain long-lasting relationships, but this is the exception, not the rule. Most of the men who adopt this life style experience numerous transitory relationships and much disappointment.

Nine.
Difficulty with
Self-Acceptance

Everyone has a problem with self-acceptance, particularly in his or her youth. Most people eventually "mature" or come to accept themselves, their talents, looks, family, etc. Those who find self-approval difficult complicate their lives. They become hesitant and insecure in their interpersonal relationships and are often avoided by others subconsciously because their manner advertises, "I don't like myself." This lack of self-acceptance also limits them vocationally and compounds every problem in their lives.

Because homosexuals suffer more rejection than others, they often have a much more difficult time with self-acceptance. Observing homosexuals in a large group at one of their haunts recently, I was struck with the fact that they seemed more "uptight" and were striving harder for acceptance than did straights in a similar situation. Although some (particularly those over thirty or thirty-five) have learned to live with and accept themselves, most homosexuals seem to fall into one of two categories. Either they are militant and angry, or they are tense and unrelaxed in social situations. Both can be the result of insecurity due to lack of self-acceptance. One of the greatest deterrents to self-acceptance in any individual is the rejection and disapproval of his parents. I will leave it to the reader to determine what percent of homosexuals enjoy the love and full acceptance of both parents. Would it be 15 to 20 percent? Certainly not more.

Ten.
Increased
Social Pressure

"The only time I can be myself is when I'm with gays," said one homosexual. He was acknowledging that life in a straight world creates all kinds of social pressure. Homosexuals complain that police are harder on them than on others, they are confronted with greater job and housing discrimination, and they become the subject of neighborhood gossip more than others. This problem, though not devastating in and of itself, heaps one more unnecessary log on the pile that makes for unhappiness in the homosexual life style.

Eleven. Increased Hostility

Unless they are bisexual, a large percentage of homosexuals reveal an excessive amount of hostility. They are particularly angry at women; some even find it difficult to carry on a working relationship with women. Last night my wife shared how she and our two sons went to an office supply store to purchase file cabinets. The clerk was extremely antagonistic to her but very forward with the boys (both in their twenties). All three independently sensed he was homosexual and made no attempt to hide it.

In interviews with homosexuals, I discovered that this anger at women can be traced to childhood, where often they were "smothered" and dominated by a love-starved mother or a dominant compulsive mother who bossed their every move. They frequently cannot relate to the opposite sex because of their inner resentments and hostility toward Mother. If the father rejected them or was a passive Milquetoast who let his wife assume his role in his child's life, the homosexual may be antagonistic toward him also. Resentment or hostility in a person's heart is a heavy burden to carry throughout life. (Many straights carry this load as well.) It can break down his health and become a major cause of ulcers, high blood pressure, heart attack, and other problems. It certainly inhibits love and emotional discipline. Anger-induced emotional reactions or decisions are consistently wrong.

Anger is a natural defense response to rejection. This could explain why many homosexuals are hostile at police "for infringing on their rights," at psychiatrists for calling them "mentally ill," at the church for labeling them "sinners," or at straights for calling them "perverts" or "deviates." If they do not learn to cope with their open or suppressed hostility toward all who oppose or disapprove of them, they will remain in a state of constant discontent. This spirit of anger, even when harbored just beneath the surface, is sensed by others, resulting in greater conflict with people and further complications. Much of the "hassle" homosexuals complain about from the straight community is caused as much by their display of hostile feelings as by society's reaction to their homosexuality.

If you think I've overstated the case, listen to this testimony of a middle-aged homosexual who opened his heart during an interview. "Usually at forty, when you're straight, you're married, with a family, a good job, and a home. Security . . . permanence. That I'd like, and it makes me . . .mad . . . that all [of] that was denied me because a bunch of idiots deciphered God and sin to suit themselves and the needs of the system." This is the man who had conceded, "I said before I have never been a happy homosexual. And I'm not going to take that back because it's true."[14]

Another illustration comes from a thirty-two-year-old analyst whose private practice consisted mainly of homosexuals. Insight into his anger appears in the statement, "I was, and am, very resentful. I resent the heterosexual stereotypical view of homosexuals (a constant complaint). I resent their thinking of us as limp-wrist faggots if we are men or truck-driver types if we are women. To be 'lumped' is offensive. I am who I am and not someone's distorted view of what they think a homosexual is. It is time heterosexuals opened their eyes and realized we are all kinds of men and women. . . ."[15]

Angry people are not happy people, and it seems that

homosexuality foments a hostile way of life.

Twelve. Vulnerability to Sadism-Masochism

Almost everyone agrees that sadism and masochism, whether practiced by a homosexual (and there are plenty of sadomasochist straights also), create a "kinky" and hazardous pattern. In the quest for "more, more, more" sex, a sadistically inclined person falls into an abusive sexual practice. We read about it when it results in murder, like the Houston thirteen, or the California trash-can murders that may account for at least twenty-four deaths. But doctors will testify that numerous cases of cuttings, slashings, whippings, and piercings go unrecorded, and only God knows how many remain untreated.

While it is true that some women are mistreated this way by sex-mad males, statistics indicate that far more than 6 percent of such crimes are committed by homosexuals. Most sado-masochism is committed by men, and it is easier for homosexual sadists to pick up a male partner. The majority of the homosexuals I have interviewed admit that their dominant fear of "cruising" for a partner is that they may be picked up by a sadist. Because of the enormous sexual promiscuity of homosexuality, the law of averages indicates that it is likely for a victim to discover too late that he is in the clutches of a sadomasochist. As one young man with his arm in a cast testified, "I was picked up two weeks ago by a sado-masochistic butch. Man, was I terrified when I realized he could kill me. I was so frightened by the weird look in his eye that I couldn't maintain an erection, and so he started beating me. I tried to run, but he slammed me to the ground and broke my arm. Maybe it was the snap of the bone or my cry of pain, but he finally left." No wonder he wanted out of that life style!

Thirteen.
Lack of a Flesh
and Blood
Family

While I was working on this manuscript, my son, his wife, and their two sons (one year and three years old) moved into our home for a month until their new house was ready for occupancy. As I watched Larry play with his boys the way I used to play with him, and as I saw the love in his eyes as he looked at them, I couldn't help contrasting that to the lonely, childless life of the homosexual. Many older homosexuals admit that they miss a family. Some are seriously interested in adopting children because they desire the fulfillment of the natural father or mother instinct. I am convinced that people suffer a distinct loss in life if they have never raised children of their own and shared themselves, their love, their dreams, and their principles for living.

God's first commandment to man clearly decreed, "Be fruitful and multiply and replenish the earth" (Gen. 1:28). It is my conviction that the Creator set our mind in its psychic mechanism, along with our instinctual traits, to function best when fulfilling that command. Lack of posterity is a serious threat to lifetime happiness. It may not seem important in one's teens and twenties, when most homosexuals embark on their sterile life style, but it becomes increasingly significant later in life. By then, however, it is usually too late. ". . . Children are a heritage of the Lord . . . Happy is the man who has his quiver full of them" (Ps. 127:3, 5). This prime area of potential happiness in life is withheld from the homosexual.

Fourteen.
The Constant
Threat of Aging

The quest for the "fountain of youth" is all but universal; everyone seems to be reluctant to grow old. But with the homosexual youth is an obsession. The entire life style is based on physical attraction. As a general pattern, the teenager is introduced to

homosexuality by a twenty- or thirty-year-old whom he
admires physically or mentally, or whose companionship he
treasures because it supplies an unrealized need in his life.
Like the ancient Greeks, who had an inordinate love for
"boys," many homosexuals would prefer sex with a young
lad. To gain that experience, they must maintain an eye appeal
of physical attractiveness. As we have seen, this drives the
"butch" to pump iron in the gymnasium, even into his sixties.
As one said, "I've got to keep this body pumped up; when it
begins to sag, I'm sexually dead, and when I'm sexually dead,
I'm dead."

The young homosexual gives little thought to the aging
problem. He goes his sexually supercharged way through the
second and third decades of life, seeking to find that "one
ultimate sexual experience." Most never find it, and although
it bothers them, it doesn't become a serious problem until
their late thirties or forties, when they experience their first
rejection. The forty-year-olds prefer twenty- and thirty-year-
old partners, but usually have to settle for fifty- and sixty-
year-olds. As one laconically mused, "Who wants an old
fag?"

If you think I'm exaggerating a side of homosexualilty that
most proponents omit, read the testimony of a newspaper
editor in his mid-sixties who appeared extremely mature in
his emotional outlook. This man loved and lived with a much
younger man with whom he did not have sex (they both feared
it would ruin their relationship), but both went out "cruising"
whenever it took their fancy. "Regarding my sex life, I put
zero effort into the chase. I am not interested in pursuing paths
that inevitably lead to rejection. And ninety-nine out of a
hundred times, the older man is rejected sexually—not only
by the young, but by the old. We are the discards, wanted by
few and feared by many. Very few people can face the
inevitable fact of their own aging. I'm not bitter about it. I
understand. I knew as I aged it would become progressively

more difficult for me sexually and socially. I accepted that. The only time I get into a self-pity rut is when I take a narrow view of me, which you can do at any age. The minute I attach more importance to sex than I should, I'm in trouble. Sex really is a much smaller part of life than most people, particularly the young, know."[16]

Later this man claimed that he had one sexual experience every six weeks or so. I couldn't help contrasting that with my seventy-five-year-old contractor friend (mentioned in *The Act of Marriage*) who claimed three lovemaking experiences per week with his wife of more than fifty years. Considered over the span of a lifetime, I'll leave it to the reader to decide who indeed has enjoyed the happier life. The reason these two men are a good comparison is that at their ages neither would win a beauty contest. One is almost sexually dead; the other lives right on because his love life is not based solely on physical attraction.

A love relationship established on personhood is not common among homosexuals. With them physical attraction predominates, and that is a transitory foundation at best. The heterosexual who gives and shares his life with another will more than likely have someone with whom to share his life in old age. However, even the homosexual who is giving and sharing his life with others will more than likely spend the last two decades of life alone and empty.

**Fifteen.
Produces Poor
Health and an
Early Death**

Dr. Daniel Cappon, a Canadian psychiatrist at the University of Toronto, has treated several hundred homosexuals. In his book *Toward an Understanding of Homosexuality*, he states,

> Homosexuality, by definition, is not healthy or wholesome.... The homosexual person, at best, will be unhappier and more unfulfilled than the

> sexually normal person. There are emotional and physical consequences to this protracted state of mental dissatisfaction. At worst, the homosexual person will die younger and suffer emotional, mental and physical illness more often than the normal person. The natural history of the homosexual person seems to be one of frigidity, impotence, broken personal relationships, psychosomatic disorders, alcoholism, paranoia psychosis, and suicide. . . . [17]

It is well known that emotional stress causes 60 to 80 percent of all illness today. Dr. S. I. McMillen in his book, *None of These Diseases,* lists fifty-one diseases caused by tension or emotional stress. Due to the social pressure placed on a homosexual person, along with the tension caused by secrecy, deceit, rejection, etc., there is no question theirs is a more emotionally pressured way of life. The human body was not designed to endure a lifetime of emotional pressure. Consequently, homosexuals will be more apt to experience illness as they grow older and probably have a shorter life span.

Sixteen. Greater Vulnerability to Depression and Suicide

Last but certainly not least, the homosexual life style is more apt to be unhappy because of the homosexual's greater vulnerability to depression and suicide than the heterosexual. In my book *How to Win Over Depression*, I cited thirteen causes of depression. The primary cause, in my opinion, is rejection of a love object. There is no question in my mind that homosexuals experience more rejection than anyone else on earth—by their parents, loved ones, God, society, and, tragically, even by homosexuals themselves. Because homosexuals are so selfish, many reject and run roughshod over the feelings of their not-so-gay friends.

Although there is no way of positively verifying it, I can
believe the suggestion that homosexuals account for 50
percent of America's suicides. In all honesty, no one knows
how many suicides occur each year. For instance, how many
of those who overdose on drugs are suicidal, and how many
auto crashes are in reality suicidal? The tremendous rejection
homosexuals experience inevitably brings them to depression
at a rate many times higher than that of the straight
community. Nothing causes suicide more than depression, for
only through an intense depression can a person be brought
to lower his self-preservation instinct to the point where he
is able to take his own life. Even if we cut the figures in half,
making the suicide rate six or seven times greater than that of
straights, it would prove my point—that "gay" isn't gay!
It is one of the world's lies that appeals to emotionally and
sexually supercharged young people with the false promise
of a "gay life." Don't you believe it! Any group characterized
by a suicide rate at least six or seven times higher than the
general public must have a similar ratio of unhappiness. All
the unhappy gays don't commit suicide; they just go from one
unhappy decade to another. But as they get older, even the
occasional exciting moments diminish, and they are left with
emptiness and depression.

Marriage and a heterosexual life style do not guarantee
perpetual happiness, as God intended, but I know many
couples who have lived joyous, fulfilled lives after thirty,
forty, and over fifty years of marriage. That rarely happens
to homosexuals. Don't let anyone tell you "gay is gay" in
later life; the burden of proof is on him! I have yet to hear one
affirm it honestly.

If these sixteen reasons don't convince you, let me just
suggest that I haven't reviewed all the evidence yet. I didn't
mention the greater degrees of jealousy, suspicion, distrust,
disloyalty, alcoholism, drugs, and other life-complicating
problems that often plague homosexuals. It is likely that I have
understated the case.

The homosexual's use of the word "gay" to describe his
life style is not just deceitful—it is a cruel hoax. As one
admitted, "Gay is a mask we homosexuals put on to disguise
the loneliness, despair and heartache we carry most of the
time."

Consider my favorite composer, whose music is loved by
millions the world over. Peter Tchaikovsky, accepted by
many as one of the world's greatest musicians, was truly a
genius, but his homosexuality brought him deep sadness and
despair. A "mama's boy" in his youth, he could not
consummate his marriage sexually and had it annulled. His
young wife felt so rejected that she went insane. He visited
her at the typical nineteenth-century sanitarium and was so
shaken by what he saw that he never forgot that dreadful sight.

Although he kept his homosexuality a secret during his less
famous days, the truth finally surfaced. Madame von Meck,
the wealthy widow who was his patron, would never meet
him personally, but a strong and dependent friendship grew
up between them through their many letters. When his
homosexuality was revealed, she severed all contact with him
and refused further support. By this time he no longer needed
her money, but the loss of her friendship plunged him into
deep despair. For ten years he experienced increasing
depressions. Eventually he visited a city where he was warned
that cholera had infected the water. Although he was not
usually a water drinker, on that one occasion he deliberately
drank profusely and died. Many think he committed suicide.

Tchaikovsky is just one in a parade of notorious
homosexuals whose lives were stalked by tragedy, sadness,
and despair. Only God knows how many of the more ordinary
homosexuals have lived tortured lives and died prematurely
because at the outset they believed the lie that homosexuality
was a "gay life."

What Causes Homosexuality?

If Kinsey was correct that 4 percent of our population really is homosexual, approximately nine to ten million people in our country have adopted this sexual preference (the Gay Lib movement likes to pump that figure up for political purposes to twenty million). But even ten million people given to that which most people throughout history have called a "perversion" requires that we carefully examine the question "Why?" What makes ninety-six people out of one hundred heterosexual and the remaining 4 percent homosexual? Few aspects of homosexuality spark more heated debate than its cause.

Are Homosexuals Born That Way?

Ever since Dr. Karl Bowman and others at the Langly Porter Clinic in San Francisco came up with the idea that a child's sexual identification is established by the time he is two and a half years of age (others say five years), it has been common for homosexuals to say, "I'm born this way" or "I can't help it." The ministerial head of the homosexual church reports, "God created me Gay." As one homosexual told me recently, "Everyone knows your sexual preference is established by the time you are five years old. Consequently, I've always been a homosexual; it's in my genes." The tragic thing about that statement is not just that it is wrong, but that it has the effect of unnecessarily binding the one who believes it into a lifetime of homosexuality. No one is born homosexual, nor is it something over which he has no control—unless he *thinks* he has no control over his sexual direction.

In spite of the assertions of the homosexual and his well-meaning friends in the academic, sociological, and media fields, not one scientific fact yet uncovered verifies that homosexuality is caused genetically, hormonally, or biologically. The evidence so overwhelmingly and so widely accepted by scientists against such a stance places the burden of proof on those who make such claims.

Biological Considerations

Without question our biological make-up exercises a profound influence on our lives. And one of the most powerful influences on one's sex drive is his hormones. When it was first discovered that both male and female hormones circulate in the bloodstream of both sexes, someone speculated that an effeminate man just had too many female hormones. Somehow, it didn't occur to him that even such a theory wouldn't explain the muscle-bound weight-lifter whose picture adorns sporting magazines but who sexually prefers men to women. Obviously his problem wasn't a lack of male hormones.

Scientists who have run extensive tests on male and female homosexuals have found their hormonal level to be the same as heterosexuals. After studying androsterone and the effects of estrogen therapy, two doctors writing in the *John Hopkins*

Medical Journal reported that "when extremely effeminate males (homosexual or heterosexual) have been tested by these means, they have shown entirely normal hormone levels."[18] Other tests have verified these findings, and some have uncovered an even higher ratio of male hormones in homosexuals than in heterosexuals. To date there is no scientific evidence to support the notion that homosexuality is inherited.

Dr. C. A. Tripp, the psychologist who wrote *The Homosexual Matrix*, stated in this connection,

> . . . a number of clinicians have seen fit over the years to run their own experiments by administering testosterone both to effeminate and to ordinary homosexuals. The results have been consistent: When there were any behavioral changes at all, the subjects became more like themselves than ever. Their sex drives were usually increased, and sometimes their effeminate mannerisms as well (when they had any), *but there were never any directional changes in their sexual interests* (author's emphasis). From these experiments, formal and informal, it has become abundantly clear that the sex hormones play a considerable role in powering human sexuality, but they do not control the direction of it.[19]

Dr. Evelyn Hooker, famous for research on homosexuality, states, "There is no evidence that homosexuals have faulty hormone levels, or that their sexual orientation can be changed with hormone injections." Dr. Charles Wahl, a researcher in this field, adds, "The vast preponderance of evidence clearly indicates that homosexuality is a learned disorder and is not genetically inherited." On the basis of all known scientific data, it is safe to say that one's genetic and biological make-up does indeed determine his sex but not his sexual preference. To answer why a small percentage of people are sexually attracted to those of their own sex, we must look beyond their biological and chemical composition to an even more complex area, their psychological makeup.

Human beings are unquestionably the most complex of all living creatures, if for no other reason than the uniqueness of the human brain. The cerebral cortex, which makes up 90 percent of our brain (compared to 40 percent in lower animals), is the most influential factor in determining our behavior. In the cerebral cortex are located our intuitions, temperament, memory, intelligence, thoughts, conscience, emotions, drives, and thinking capabilities. This complex computer-like mechanism receives, records, processes, and organizes every experience we have, beginning even before birth. The cerebral cortex separates man universally from the animal kingdom and is responsible for almost all of his behavior. Particularly is that true of his sexual expression. A person's psychological makeup is "the bent" or direction of life his cerebral cortex motivates him to take, based on the net result of all life experiences and teachings.

A simple illustration of that would involve two identical twins. Actually, it is impossible to find two exactly identical temperaments, intellects, senses, etc. even in two identical bodies, but for illustration we will assume we can. If one of our identical twins were placed in a criminal's home at birth, where he was unwanted, neglected, persecuted, taught criminality, and left to fend for himself, he would develop a criminal psychological makeup that would lead him into a life of crime. He would probably grow up to lie, cheat, steal, and even kill without the slightest twinge of conscience. His identical brother, placed in a loving, law-abiding home, showered with affection balanced by discipline, and taught Christian principles to live by, would grow up with a moral psychological outlook. In either case his behavior would be the outcome or result of his psychological makeup.

Consider now two other identical twins, with all the same

components but raised in different homes. One is homosexual,
the other heterosexual. Why? One has developed a
homosexual psychological mental attitude while the other
has cultivated a heterosexual mental attitude. You might well
ask, is sexual expression a matter of the mind, a mental
attitude? Absolutely! As explained in *The Act of Marriage*,
a person's most important sex organ is his *brain*! If your
brain is conditioned to respond to opposite sex stimuli, you
will. If it is conditioned to respond to same-sex stimuli, it
will. At first that sounds simple—but don't be misled.
Conditioning a person to function contrary to his natural sex
impulses is very complex, for a number of factors induce
a person to develop a predisposition toward his own sex.
And even then most of the people with such a predisposition
do not become homosexual. Basically, then, there are two
causes of homosexuality: 1) a homosexual psychological
outlook (what psychologists usually term "a predisposition"
toward homosexuality) and 2) a learned behavior. In some
cases both are present. In an increasing number of people
only the latter is necessary to develop a lifetime habit of
homosexuality. We shall examine both of these causes
carefully.

A Predisposition
to Homosexuality

The formula on page 77 graphically diagrams the
major factors that cause a normal boy or girl to grow up with
"a predisposition toward their own sex." This predilection
usually occurs so early in life that the person thinks it is born
in him when really it is formed in him. No one is born
homosexual, but if enough of the wrong components are
present, he will *gradually* develop a predisposition toward
it. All of the wrong components are not required to produce
a homosexual tendency. Perhaps the "degree of

homosexuality'' observed by psychologists is determined by how many of the following ingredients are present in a person's background.

One. Temperament

The most powerful single influence on a person's behavior is his inherited temperament. And since homosexuality is a behavior pattern, it follows that a person's temperament will play a significant role in determining whether or not he develops a predisposition toward homosexuality. As we have noted, homosexuality is a learned behavior, but some people find it easier to learn than others. As we shall see, that is because of their temperament.

Dr. C. A. Tripp concurs: " . . . disposition and temperament unquestionably affect the ease with which individual experience stamps itself into a person's total register. (Thus there are sizable differences in how easily people can be conditioned in any direction)."[20] Dr. James D. Mallory, psychiatrist and director of the Atlanta Counseling Center, states, "Some studies do suggest that temperament is inherited—and I would suspect there often is a biological predisposing vulnerability to homosexuality. New-born infants who are kickers and screamers, 15 to 20 years from now still are kicking and screaming. And a passive infant 15 to 20 years from now still tends to be passive."[21]

The theory of the four temperaments, first conceived by Hippocrates 2400 years ago, is the oldest concept of human behavior on record. Although considered unfashionable by Freud and his followers, it is gradually coming back into contention as a viable explanation to why man acts the way he does. The careful analyzer of people will find that they fall into basic behavioral categories. Although some of this behavior can rightfully be traced to culture, environment, training (or lack of training), education, role example, and other factors, an extremely significant aspect is inherited temperament. A growing number of anthrobiologists are being attracted to a new science called "sociobiology," which attributes 10 to 15 percent of a person's behavior to genetic input. Those who accept the four temperaments theory teach that temperament is passed on from parents to their children through the genes. This is the first building block in constructing human behavior. The four temperaments are as follows: (1) Sanguine: the lively, active, fun-loving, natural-born superextrovert salesman; (2) Choleric: the hard-driving, strong-willed, extrovert-leader, promoter, crusader; (3) Melancholy: the sensitive, artistic, gifted, introvert-perfectionist; and (4) Phlegmatic: the easy-going superintrovert who diplomatically lives without offending others. As I explain in detail in my latest book, *Understanding the Male Temperament*, no individual contains one of these temperaments exclusively, for we are all a blend of at least two. One temperament will predominate, the other remaining secondary. A 60 percent Sanguine and 40 percent Phlegmatic is a "SanPhleg"; a 70 percent Choleric and 30 percent Melancholy is known as a "ChlorMel." In all there are at least twelve possible blends. (For a complete study of the four temperaments, please consult one of the author's three books on the subject.)*

It has been my observation that most homosexuals reflect a high degree of Melancholy temperament—not always, of course, but to a large degree. That is not to say that other temperaments do not also produce homosexuals, for I have met some representing each temperament. However, the majority I have encountered have been predominantly Melancholy; next was Phlegmatic, Sanguine, then a few Cholerics. Six temperament blends are more vulnerable to a predisposition to homosexuality than others: MelPhleg,

---

Understanding the Male Temperament, Spirit-Controlled Temperament, and *Transformed Temperaments.*

MelSan, MelChlor, PhlegMel, SanMel, and ChlorMel.
Although I would not be dogmatic, it would be my judgment
that three-fourths or more of the homosexual population,
both male and female, have a MelPhleg, MelSan, or
MelChlor temperament. The other three blends mentioned
will make up most of the rest.

Please bear in mind, I am *not* saying that all Melancholies
are homosexual. I am not even suggesting that most
Melancholies have a predisposition toward homosexuality.
But I do maintain that most of those with a predisposition
toward homosexuality are of the Melancholy temperament.
A reasonable "guesstimate" would be that 25 percent of the
total population is predominantly Melancholy; if another
25 percent is secondarily Melancholy, and 4 to 5 percent of
the population is homosexual, then it follows that about 10
percent of those with a Melancholy temperament may have a
tendency toward homosexuality. But remember, even if we
estimated that as high as 20 to 25 percent of the Melancholy
temperaments in our population had a predisposition toward
homosexuality, that would still mean that the vast majority
(the other 75 to 80 percent) of those who inherited a
Melancholy temperament are *not* homosexual, nor do they
have a predisposition toward it.

Admittedly, the above-mentioned percentages are highly
speculative, but the observation that most of the homosexuals
I have interviewed possess either a primary or secondary
Melancholy temperament is not speculation.

The preponderance of Melancholy temperaments among
homosexuals accounts for several factors in the study of
homosexuality heretofore unresolved. It explains why Ellis
and others made the mistake of thinking that homosexuality
was a "sign of greatness." It would be more accurate to
say that the Melancholy temperament is a sign of potential
greatness. Most of the world's geniuses had a Melancholy
temperament: such great composers as Bach, Beethoven,

Schubert, Wagner, Mozart, Tchaikovsky; great artists like Michelangelo, van Gogh, Rembrandt, and others; gifted sculptors, scientists, inventors, philosophers, musicians, writers, etc. They were all predominantly Melancholy in temperament; that is why they were so creative. The fact that a few were homosexual does not mean that their homosexuality occasioned their greatness. It would be more accurate to say that their Melancholy temperament determined their greatness, but it also gave some of them a predisposition toward homosexuality. Their home life as small children further enhanced this possibility.

Consider the characteristics of the Melancholy temperament carefully; if you know a homosexual, you will find that he shares many of them. Melancholies are sensitive, gifted perfectionists who often possess an analytical bent of mind. They are idealists with a love for music and the fine arts. Compared to Cholerics and Sanguines, a Melancholy temperament sees in three-dimensional technicolor and hears in quadraphonic sound. They are without doubt the most creative of all temperaments. Unfortunately, no temperament is without its own set of weaknesses which will limit the use of its potential strengths. In the case of Melancholies, they are apt to be moody, negative, critical, self-centered, touchy, persecution-prone, revengeful, legalistic, rigid, unsociable, theoretical, and impractical. This combination of strengths and weaknesses usually produces a capable person who is insecure about himself or his abilities. It also explains an observation about people that I made years ago, and which time and observation have confirmed: the most naturally talented people tend to be the least sure of themselves, and they usually undersell their capabilities. I have noted that most Melancholy men, even those firmly heterosexual, are not relaxed around women. Actually, they aren't apt to be relaxed and self-confident about anything—except the area of their gift, like music or

art, which they have practiced repeatedly and in which they
have developed assurance. This basic insecurity possibly
tends to make them unsure about the opposite sex and find
comfort in pursuits with their own sex.

There are so many homosexuals in clothing design, hair
dressing, interior decoration, art, music, ballet, acting,
TV producing, newspaper and magazine work, writing,
education, and other similar vocations because those fields
usually require people with a predominantly (or at least
secondary) Melancholy temperament. And as we have seen,
some people with a Melancholy temperament have a greater
tendency toward homosexuality than people of other
temperament groups.

Have you noticed how supportive the arts and media are
of the homosexual movement today? The ridicule of Anita
Bryant by prominent movie, opera, and TV personalities
is a case in point. Some have been outspokenly derogatory
toward her and the cause she leads to protect our children
from having homosexual school teachers as role models. I am
not suggesting that those stars are all homosexual, but some
admittedly are; others are "closet gays" (that is why people
have to be careful whom they listen to on this subject; some
advocates of homosexuality are only protecting their secret
life style), and almost all have many homosexual friends with
whom they work every day. Heterosexuals who defend
homosexuality as an optional life style usually don't really
know what is going on in the homosexual community, nor
do they realize the sadness homosexuality engenders. You
would think they would become suspicious due to the higher
suicide rate among homosexuals, but the swinging set prides
itself on being "tolerant." Unfortunately, tolerance toward
the homosexual mandates intolerance toward the innocent
school children Anita Bryant is concerned about. If her
program is not successful, millions of children will be

unnecessarily swept into the homosexual life style. This realistic possibility forces us to ask who is *really* being tolerant—the pro-homosexuality crowd or Anita Bryant?

Returning again to the subject of temperament, I would like to reinforce my statement that not all those with predominant Melancholy temperaments in the arts, etc., are homosexual. I introduced the concept here not to embarrass or burden people with a Melancholy temperament, but to encourage parents of Melancholy children to go out of their way to love them. I have noticed that every homosexual I have encountered or have discussed with other counselors possesses an enormous hunger for love. This powerful drive to love and to attract love is typical not only of homosexuals but of Melancholies.

Two. Inadequate Parental Relationships

Parents are easily the most important external force in the life of any child and, as would be suspected, contribute largely to the homosexual or heterosexual predisposition of their children. A professor of psychiatry at one of the nation's leading medical schools stated, "Current research indicates that the family most likely to produce a homosexual comprises a very intimate, possessive and dominating mother and a detached, hostile father. Many mothers of lesbians tend to be hostile and competitive with their daughters. The fathers of female homosexuals seldom appear to play a dominant role in the family and have considerable difficulty being openly affectionate with their daughters."

Most of the new books on homosexuality contain the report by Dr. Irving Bieber, who studied the family backgrounds of 106 male homosexuals. According to his discoveries, eighty-one mothers were dominating, sixty-two were overprotective, sixty-six made the homosexual their favorite child, eighty-two of the fathers spent very little time with their sons, and seventy-nine maintained a detached attitude toward them.[22]

As important as the father is in the life of a child, even he must take second place to mother during the first three years of life. She feeds the baby at her breast and spends far more time with him in infancy than does his dad. Consequently, mothers actually have more to do with producing a predisposition toward homosexuality than fathers. Two kinds of mothers are particularly harmful—smother mothers and dominating mothers.

Smother Mothers

Every child needs love, but few things are worse than an overprotective, smothering affection that is showered on an infant, not for his benefit but for the mother's. Many a love-starved young mother satisfies her love hunger on her child until he is the primary object in her life. The more she bestows her affection, time, and attention on her child, the more she neglects her husband. This may turn him further from her and the child, compounding the problem.

Dr. Howard Hendricks used to say in Family Seminars which he and I held together that "whenever a mother makes her son number one in her life, she begins to raise a pervert." In other words, it is normal for a boy to be number two in the heart of his mother, for he doesn't feel threatened when he knows father is number one. But when mother and father cannot preserve a love relationship and she makes the child number one, he is in trouble. He may begin to identify with her, take an interest in feminine things, and develop effeminate mannerisms. Such concerns start early in life and are very difficult to break. One veteran homosexual in the counseling room complained that his mother was "overprotective and smothering." He illustrated the latter by saying, "She never hesitated to embarrass me. She thought nothing of unzipping my pants to tuck in my shirt. Between that and wiping my nose, she was all over me."

Throughout history, researchers have repeatedly verified that homosexuals are "mama's boys" whose mothers doted on them in their youth. Tchaikovsky, Michelangelo, and Freud are notable examples. Insecure mothers who have a need to be needed take out that compulsion on their infant or small child to the detriment of the child's personality. Some call it love, but it is not! In reality, it is a form of selfishness, and it probably constitutes one of the leading causes in the rise of homosexuality.

In recent years it has become fashionable for an unwed mother who heeds the advice of sexual permissivists to raise her child alone. I always wince when I see this, not because a mother can't raise her son alone (my brother and I were raised by a widowed mother, and my brother was only seven weeks old when Father died, so I know it can be done), but most of those girls have the wrong motive. They are usually love-starved girls who want something living to love and often end up "smother loving" a child into a predisposition toward homosexuality.

Dominant Mothers

One of the sociological phenomena of our times is the enormous increase in the dominant role of the mother and the renunciation by the father of his responsibility to lead. In some cases dominance is forced upon women because of an irresponsible husband. But nothing ruins the sexual adjustment of children more surely than an oppressive wife and mother. Such children build up an intense hostility toward the opposite sex that either makes it difficult for them to

show love and affection in marriage or creates a predisposition
toward homosexuality.

A Passive
or Absent Father

Father may only be the secondary influence in the life of his
children, but since he is second in importance, we should
consider him carefully. I have never counseled a homosexual,
read one's case history, heard another counselor discuss a
client, or listened to the testimony of a former homosexual
but that I was informed that the deviant had either a bad
relationship with his father or none at all. No doubt some
homosexual somewhere has climbed over the positive force of
his father's love and masculine role example to become
homosexual, but in the many cases I have studied, I cannot
name *one*. A father's most precious gift to his son or daughter
is not food, shelter, and education, but love—and he must
prove that love by spending time with his child.

A former homosexual, now a minister who is effectively
helping homosexuals out of their life style, relates a most
traumatic childhood experience that shows the importance
of the father. Long before he ever felt a "twinge of
homosexuality," he was out in the garage with his father,
overhauling the car. From under the car came the
commanding voice, "Hand me the crescent wrench." He had
no idea what a crescent wrench was, so he replied, "I can't
find it." His hostile father erupted in an angry spirit, sprang
to his feet, and located it in clear view. Cuffing his son on the
side of the head, he called him a vile name, rebuked him for
being so stupid, and shouted, "Go into the house and help
your mother with the girls' work. You obviously aren't cut out
for a man's job." When a small boy's father claims he is more
girl-like than male, what is he to believe? Today, having

shed the homosexual practices of many agonizing years, this man is still effeminate in his mannerisms, but he struggles valiantly to be accepted as "straight."

Father's love and approval of his manhood is very important to any boy, particularly one who manifests other tendencies which may develop a predisposition toward homosexuality. Dr. Irvin Bieber, a psychiatrist acclaimed by the *Miami Herald* as "one of the most authoritative students of homosexuality in America," said, "Homosexuals are not born that way; they are made that way largely by their parents."

According to a nationally known psychiatrist, the background of homosexuals fits a common pattern. Father is frequently absent from the home, and thus Mother turns to the boy as an outlet for her emotional needs. A boy needs to identify with his father's masculinity; we need to bring Father back into the home, and the father and son must spend time together. A former homosexual who has carried on an effective ministry for five years among homosexuals reported, "I have counseled over three hundred homosexuals and have yet to find one that enjoyed a warm love relationship with his father."

The best way to stamp out homosexuality in this country is for parents to get back to the business of making parenthood their priority. Children raised in loving, well-disciplined homes where Mother and Father are themselves good role models for their children rarely become homosexual. Unfortunately, unloved children subjected to the selfish neglect of their parents are vulnerable to a predisposition toward homosexuality. This year divorce may reach 1,100,000, bringing to eleven million the number of children to be raised by one parent. It is estimated that because of divorce, twenty-five to thirty million children up to eighteen years of age will spend a portion of their childhood raised by one parent.

A psychiatrist told me, "Every homosexual I know has come from a broken home." My own experience is not that conclusive but I have found that every homosexual I know came from an unhappy home where fighting and hatred abounded between the parents, who usually proceeded with a divorce.

Three. Permissive Childhood Training

The most harmful concept in the field of child raising during the past 100 years has been permissiveness. It is hard to believe that such a destructive doctrine could catch on so quickly and sweep the country with such force. Although thoroughly discredited now, it has wrought havoc on millions. Perhaps its popularity can be attributed to the fact that the discipline of children is burdensome to parents. But only parental discipline will enable young people to grow up to become responsible, self-disciplined adults.

A recent study of criminals indicated that those individuals treated to a well-moderated program of love and discipline in their youth reflected the lowest tendency toward crime. Interestingly enough, the same would be true of homosexuals. I have found in digging into their backgrounds that they were either rejected or pampered as children. I have met only one homosexual who was not a self-indulgent, self-centered, undisciplined individual. The only motivation that seems to make them forceful is their pursuit of sexual gratification and their demand to be accepted by society as "perfectly normal." This lack of discipline makes it easy for many with a predisposition toward homosexuality to take up the practice at the first opportunity, and it is largely the reason they find it so difficult to extricate themselves from it when they finally wake up to the realization it is an "ungay" life style.

THE COMPONENTS FOR DEVELOPING A HOMOSEXUAL DISPOSITION

Melancholy Temperament

+

Permissive Childhood
Training

+

Insecurity
about Sexual Identity

+

Childhood
Sexual Experiences

+

Early Interest
in Sex

+

Youthful Masturbator
and Sexual Fantasizer

―――――――――――――――――――

A Predisposition toward Homosexuality*

*It should be kept in mind that most of those with a predisposition toward homosexuality have never had a homosexual experience, and more than 80 percent of those who have such a predisposition *are not homosexual*.

Four.
Insecurity about
Sexual Identity

Many case studies and reports indicate confusion about homosexuals' sexual identity as preschoolers. It is well known that unwise parents have psychologically damaged their children by rejecting their sex. A father, for example, may have given his little girl a name like Roberta or Stephanie, not because he liked the name, but because he had expected a boy and intended to call him Robert or Stephen. Recently I met an attractive blond, blue-eyed woman named "Karleen." Her German father wanted a boy he could name Karl. Fortunately, she outgrew the ill effects of trying desperately to act like a boy to please her father. The same is true of boys whose parents wanted a girl baby. Somehow this sexual rejection is passed on to the children, and it tends to make them reject their own sex and try to imitate the opposite sex, which creates tension and frustration because it is unnatural. Consequently, though they may take on effeminate or tomboy characteristics and relate socially with the opposite sex, it makes it more difficult for them to relate sexually, for they think of themselves as members of that opposite sex. Although most such children eventually grow up to be heterosexual, some are so threatened by this confused sex role that they identify excessively with their own sex. In extreme cases they hate their own genitals because they keep them from being the opposite sex. This is one of the causes of transsexual operations.

It is important for girls to accept their femininity and enjoy being women, while boys should be trained to esteem their manhood. Learning to love and accept yourself is fundamental to learning to love someone else. Everyone starts out life insecure to some degree, but "growing up" means learning to accept yourself and other people. Insecurity about one's sexuality will make it difficult for him to accept himself.

**Five.
Childhood
Sexual Trauma**

Until we talk to homosexuals about the intimate details of their lives, it is almost impossible for most of us to imagine some of the bizarre things adults have done to innocent little children. The sexual molestation of children is more often perpetrated by heterosexuals than by homosexuals (after all, 95 percent of the population is heterosexual), and statistics indicate that fathers or stepfathers who commit incest with their daughters are the most frequent offenders. Such activity often creates psychological complexes that make children "hate sex" in later life. Many of these victims marry and raise a family but develop sexual problems that disturb or ruin their sex life. It is not at all uncommon to hear lesbians describe a basic hatred for men—learned because of a molesting father.

Little boys are often subject to even more potential sexual traumas than little girls because so many parents are naive in discounting the perverse capabilities of men. One homosexual told his counselor, "My earliest recollection in life is of sucking a man's penis through the bars of my crib." During the time he was two or three years old his mother took in boarders, and one evidently had a perverted disrespect for children. Many little boys are introduced to masturbation by babysitters long before they go to school, and some have been introduced to homosexuality. The "nice little boy down the street" may not really be such a nice little boy.

Childhood is a time of curiosity, and that certainly involves sex. Little boys are particularly prone to sexual curiosity and experimentation. Many homosexuals acknowledge that their initial homosexual experience with another boy or group of boys occurred because of peer pressure. Whatever the reason, such an experience can start a guilt pattern, a habit, or thought process which produces a predisposition toward homosexuality.

Parents can inadvertently contribute to this problem also. Many a sensitive homosexual was "turned off" toward heterosexual relationships because his parents were not discreet in their lovemaking, and failed to shield their small children from witnessing sexual intimacy before they were old enough to understand. It is traumatic for children to see any two people experiencing sex, but particularly their parents. Fear of the unknown is psychologically harmful, especially in childhood. No wonder the Bible cautions parents against permitting their children to see their nakedness.

Human sexuality is easily one of the most mysterious and exciting of life's experiences. Premature sexual experiences, whether entered into voluntarily or forcibly, are almost always harmful, particularly to children. Sex is basically an adult experience, for children are not psychologically equipped to handle it—even if they have the physical capacity. The closer a child gets to puberty, the more dangerous are premature sexual experiences.

Six. Early Interest in Sex

Long before the serious research for this book began, it occurred to me that many homosexuals displayed an interest in sex at an incredibly early age. This study has confirmed that impression, revealing that sexual contacts often occurred much earlier than I had imagined. Some homosexuals have confided that they first masturbated or had homosexual experiences at five years of age. Frankly, I was dubious, but several case studies and reports verify this. Dr. Tripp states that researchers involved in the Kinsey program detected a sexual precociousness in homosexual males.

> And not only do homosexual males tend to arrive at puberty early, they tend to start masturbating much earlier (and continue it more extensively the rest of their lives) than do males who are less early

and less active sexually. Conversely, males
who belong to that portion of the population
which arrives at puberty relatively late tend
to be less active sexually and are
extraordinarily prone to being entirely
heterosexual.[23]

Sexual stimulation, which clearly stems from a variety of
sources, particularly in boys, can bring on an early fascination
with sex. A boy may respond with vigorous erections to many
forms of excitement like anger, riding a horse or bicycle,
etc. As he gets older, this excitement will change to sexual
stimulation, particularly after puberty. However, if he finds
erections exciting, and if he or his friends learn to produce
the stimulation necessary for erection before puberty, this
can be very dangerous because it does not have a natural
direction to take. Consequently, since most of his intimate
friends at this age are boys, this early sex drive moves him in a
same-sex direction and he becomes vulnerable to
homosexuality.

Because many homosexuals were "mama's boys," some
researchers are suspicious that "smother mothers"
inadvertently stimulate their sons by intimate expressions
of affection. Once aroused, homosexual interest must take
some direction. It is unthinkable that it be toward his mother,
and at his age other boys afford the only alternative. As
unpleasant as the thought may be, it is entirely logical that
mothers can unknowingly force a premature interest in sex
and thus create in their sons a predisposition toward
homosexuality.

**Seven.
Youthful
Masturbator
and Sexual
Fantasizer**

Almost every homosexual I have
counseled or studied has been an
early and heavy masturbator. In fact,
masturbation seems to be the first
sexual step toward homosexuality.
Further, almost every masturbator is
a fantasizer. Although I have been criticized for teaching in

my book *The Act of Marriage* that masturbation and
fantasizing are harmful, I am even more convinced of that
fact after this study. Most professional counselors teach that
sexual fantasies are harmless, and even some Christian
counselors endorse masturbation because it is not expressly
condemned in the Bible. Mental lust, however, was
condemned by Jesus Christ and compared to adultery.
Recently some psychologists have begun to recognize the
dangers of youthful fantasies while masturbating.

Dr. Tripp stated,

> A considerable body of data indicates that
> boys who begin masturbating early (usually
> before puberty) while simultaneously
> looking at their own genitalia can build a
> crucial associative connection between
> maleness, male genitalia, and all that is
> sexually valuable and exciting. These
> associations amount to an eroticism which
> is "ready" to extend itself to other male
> attributes, particularly to those of a later
> same-sex partner. This associative pattern
> sometimes manages to preempt
> heterosexual interests, not only by coming
> first but by vitalizing a nearby thought
> chain most boys entertain to some extent:
> that since girls have no penis, they are
> sexless and thus sexually uninteresting.
> This whole line of development in which
> maleness is the target as well as the gun of
> sex is no mere invention of armchair
> theorists. Its reality is supported by an
> impressive amount of parallel evidence.[24]

In all probability the boy who masturbates early in life and
fantasizes about himself or other males before he is interested
in the opposite sex does so because he has already developed
a predisposition toward homosexuality. This practice seems to
serve as the catalyst that diverts him to the mental attitude of
homosexuality.

Eight.
Childhood
Associates and
Peer Pressure

The influence of one child upon another is far greater than most adults realize. Many parents let their children play with neighborhood youngsters, giving little or no thought to the fact that they may be placing them in a grossly immoral environment.

The influence of children upon each other is twofold: peer pressure and bad example. A child from a broken home provides a classic illustration. His parents wanted a little girl and communicated that to his older brother and sister, who teased him about being a girl unceasingly until he tried to be one. At seventeen he wanted to change his sex surgically because he was convinced he should have been a girl. Everything that reminded him of being a boy turned him off. He wanted so desperately to please his mother and older brother and sister that he had psychologically castrated himself. Complete hormonal tests proved nothing abnormal in his glands, but his mind was so fixed on being female that he could not function as a male. Such a person is easily swept into homosexuality.

Many feminine-acting homosexual males testify to intense teasing and ridicule as children growing up. When peers say, "You're a sissy, you can't play football or baseball," a child tends to believe it. If he has been rejected by his father and has no male role image to imitate in the home, and if his mother has "smothered" him, all it takes for him to think of himself as a "queen" is teasing by his peers. Instead of developing more masculine traits as he bumps into the cruel world around him, his feminine tendencies are accentuated. "You are what you think you are," and if your peers convince you that you're a queen, then you're a queen. When his sex drive begins to awaken, such a teen-ager can easily be enticed into the homosexual life style.

The other factor that contributes to a homosexual predisposition induced by one's peers is childhood experimentation and bad examples. Boys are more inclined to be sexual exhibitionists and experimenters than girls, although bored teen-age girls have taught unbelievably advanced sex habits to little girls long before unsuspecting parents realized it. With almost one-third of the nation's mothers working today, plus women's involvement in many other activities in this highly mobile age, small children are cared for by persons other than their mothers for long periods of time daily. It doesn't take a lesbian baby-sitter to teach a small child bad habits. If a young girl is subject to sexual curiosity and a few "back alley" thoughts, an older girl can experiment on her until she learns or observes experiences that no child should be subjected to. Such events do nothing to stabilize a girl's sexual development into a normal young lady.

Because of their stronger sex drive, boys tend to get into experimentation groups voluntarily. Most homosexuals admit to sexual experimentation with other boys early in their teens. Usually one or more of the boys is older and leads the younger ones into group masturbation. Some reports even tell of teen contests to see who could ejaculate the farthest or fastest. If a boy meets with this group often enough, "sodomy" experimentation (anal insertion) is almost sure to take place eventually. Even though the experience may seem distasteful at first, strong peer pressure at that age will persuade him to submit.

Although such behavior may seem bizarre to naive heterosexual parents, it is life in the real world for many young people today. Particularly in crowded cities where work is unavailable, life is boring and many teens have been taught no moral principles by either word or example. What makes such irregular behavior so dangerous is the age at which it takes place, probably early or middle teens—or even

earlier. At this time boys should be supremely interested in
sports and educational activities, but sexual experimentation
becomes so exciting that they often lose interest in everything
else. Easy access to pornographic literature, much of which
panders to homosexuality, accelerates the process. It is
dangerous for boys to engage in sexual practices with their
own sex prior to and during the time they should begin to show
interest in girls, for they develop an appetite for their own
sex and a predisposition toward homosexuality.

Predisposition Summary

What is a predisposition toward homosexuality? Simply
defined, it is a tendency to experience a greater sexual
attraction toward one's own sex than toward the opposite sex.
It is not homosexuality *per se*, though it may lead a person
into homosexuality. Again I would insist that the majority of
men and women with a predisposition toward homosexuality
did not take up homosexuality as a life style but married and
learned to be completely heterosexual. Some of the latter
group do indicate occasional attraction to a person of their
own sex, but because of moral convictions, family
responsibility, or just plain faithfulness to their spouses, they
never respond to these feelings, which soon pass when not
cultivated.

Extensive discussion among counselors and scientists about
the predisposition toward homosexuality verifies that it is a
very complex matter. Keep in mind, not any of the eight steps
just described will develop a predisposition toward
homosexuality, but a combination can. Millions of people
have one or two of these patterns in their background but
are completely heterosexual today. Others may even add a
few childhood homosexual experiences to one or two of the
steps but at present have no predisposition toward

homosexuality. For that reason I strongly suspect that it would take several of the steps to give a person a strong propensity toward it. Unfortunately, except for temperament, many of the other steps seem to travel in groups.

Since this is a highly speculative field of observation, I am reluctant to be dogmatic on my next point, but it does seem to me that the strength or degree of a person's predisposition toward homosexuality depends on how many of the above steps were active in his background, how frequently they occurred, and how strong the events were. For example, an individual whose secondary temperament is Melancholy, whose father fluctuated between affection and rejection, whose mother had several children whom she "smothered" with affection, who had only one traumatic sexual experience and a moderate amount of masturbatory fantasizing would probably be only mildly predisposed toward homosexuality. On the other hand, a person whose primary temperament was Melancholy, whose father rejected him completely, who was "smothered by mother" and who developed a precocious pattern of masturbatory fantasizing could develop a strong predisposition toward homosexuality even without some of the other steps listed. In either case, a predisposition toward homosexuality is developed in childhood, not genetically infused, and it appears in varying degrees.

Predispositioned but Not Homosexual

It should also be kept in mind that a predisposition toward homosexuality is *not* synonymous with homosexuality. Many very normal heterosexuals have experienced all eight steps in their background and yet are not homosexuals. Although it is impossible to know for certain, it would seem that about 50 percent of today's population can point to from three to five of the eight steps to such a predisposition in their background, yet only about 5 percent of them are homosexuals today. That means quite clearly that having a predisposition toward homosexuality does not make a person homosexual, nor does it even create a drive within him which he cannot control. If he does not cultivate that drive or predisposition, he will never become a homosexual.

Homosexuality Is a Learned Behavior

In spite of the cries of the homosexual community that "I'm born this way," "I can't help it," "God made me this way," or "I've always been different," homosexuality is a learned behavior, the result of individual choice. There is no evidence that anyone has ever been forced against his will to become homosexual. He may be forcibly raped or "sodomized," but that certainly doesn't make him a homosexual. It could, however, if he lets his mind fantasize favorably about same-sex experiences. A case in point is prison life, where homosexuality is rampant and many a newcomer is raped publicly as a show of strength by the reigning macho butch. It is not uncommon for a man to be used many times in prison, but as soon as he is released, revert to a heterosexual life style. The reason? Same-sex fantasies did not fill his mind.

Sexual feelings after puberty are normal. But if those feelings are not controlled, sexual permissiveness will become rampant and human beings will function sexually like animals. While we may not be able to control the existence of sexual feelings as adults, we certainly can govern their intensity, expression, and direction. That is where the mind comes in, for nothing pours emotional gasoline on our feelings like our mind.

The point has already been made that most homosexuals acknowledge an early practice of fantasizing sexual acts. This is probably the most influential factor in directing their sexual expression. (It is also the most profound influence on one's sexual intensity.) I have found that homosexuals are almost universally heavy readers of pornographic books—and, as you would suspect, of the homosexual variety. In fact, the more sexually obsessed they are, the more given they are to reading homosexual pornography. Anyone can see that homosexuality has increased in direct proportion to the increase in pornography. The danger of any kind of pornography lies in the lurid imaginations it creates in the reader's mind, lingering long after the book is destroyed.

Once a person fantasizes sex with a member of his own sex, it is easier to do it again. If he reads and looks at pictures about it, he will feel like doing it. And though he still hasn't become homosexual by engaging in a homosexual activity, *it is easier to visualize* and thus anticipate a pleasurable experience. The more he does it, the more the habit is formed and the more entrenched his homosexual thinking and fantasizing become. That is why it is easier for a young homosexual to be cured than for an old one, even though the young person has the stronger sex drive. His thought patterns are just not as deeply entrenched.

"Straights" are concerned about homosexual teachers being given the opportunity to extol homosexuality as an honorable life style in their classrooms, for such teachings can create in a child's mind positive thought patterns toward homosexuality. Without any positive direction toward this life style, the young person after puberty naturally begins thinking and feeling sexually toward the opposite sex. But if homosexual thought patterns become entrenched in a child's mind before puberty, his increased sex drive after puberty will intensify in that direction rather than redirect him to the opposite sex. Remember, the body is the servant of the mind —and the mind can be conditioned and directed. That is particularly true of wrong sex images before puberty.

Not only young people can "learn" this mental same-sex pattern. All sexual feelings are exciting, and to inexperienced young people past puberty they may even be quite alarming. Boys feel more relaxed around boys, and that is one reason they may drift into experimentation with group masturbation. The danger of this or homosexuality on any basis is that it causes the mind to think excitedly and develop a keen appetite for one's own sex when it should be directed at the opposite sex. When a boy becomes enamored sexually with the male strength, toughness, and genitalia instead of with female curves, softness, and mystique, he has been thinking for some time in that direction and is conditioning his mind to become homosexual. Such thoughts sooner or later will lead to a homosexual experience, which is not difficult to obtain today, and this further establishes his homosexual thinking patterns. This has nothing to do with hormones or glands, but it has everything to do with the direction he permits his thoughts and fantasies to take.

Dr. John White, having had homosexual experiences, explains,

> Once I experience physical pleasure with a member of my own sex, I am more likely to want to experience it again. The more frequently I experience it, the more fixed will the pattern become. What I do determines what I am just as much as what I am determines what I do.[25]

Dr. White points out that in his experience, homosexuals who want to change can marry and set in motion a chain reaction in which heterosexual experience gradually increases their ability to experience heterosexual pleasures. But that will be true only when they refuse to let their minds indulge in homosexual fantasy while engaging in heterosexual activities. Homosexuals who continue fantasies almost always return to homosexuality regardless of their good intentions, promises, or even marriage. We are what we think. But we often fail to realize that we can control our feelings by controlling our thoughts. If we don't, they can destroy us.

According to Dr. C. A. Tripp,

> There are adolescents (and a few late-arriving adults) who begin having homosexual experiences which at first may have little appeal and only gradually become meaningful. (The same could be said for the way many people develop heterosexual tastes.) This is the conditioning-by-experience which public opinion anticipates in its attitudes toward the seduction of minors. And the same idea is reflected in the homosexual adage, "Today's trade is tomorrow's competition".... It is as if sexual practice by itself can establish a pattern which then becomes self-motivating.[26]

Homosexuals are made, not born! They are made by thinking positively toward homosexual practices, then participating in such practices, which in turn provides pleasure and leads consequently to more positive thoughts toward homosexuals which lead to increased homosexual activity, until the individual's sexual thoughts and expressions are exclusively homosexual. As his thoughts and activities become more same-sex oriented, he tends to think negatively about the opposite sex. Subsequently any suggestion to a homosexual that he become more interested in girls is repugnant. Why? His mind is obsessed with his own sex.

It is obvious from this formula that a predisposition toward homosexuality itself does not implement it. Homosexuality requires an initial experience followed by same-sex thought patterns and more experiences. What causes an ordained minister, married, and the father of two children to announce to his wife one day, "I am leaving you; I'm homosexual"? He may have developed a predisposition toward homosexuality and had some homosexual experiences before

THE FORMULA FOR
PRODUCING A HOMOSEXUAL

A Predisposition
Toward Homosexuality

+

That First
Homosexual Experience

×

Pleasurable and Positive
Homosexual Thoughts

+

More Homosexual
Experiences

×

More Pleasurable
Thoughts

_____

A Homosexual

marriage, but after the wedding he probably fantasized such thoughts until he no longer found heterosexual activities with his wife appealing, so he cultivated a homosexual life style. He can proclaim from the housetops, "God made me gay," but in actuality he permitted his thoughts to drift into homosexual fantasies until "the meditations of his heart" made him gay. Homosexual fantasies produce homosexual appetites that lead to homosexual experiences.

Homosexuals tell me, "Homosexuality is more exciting than heterosexuality." That is utter nonsense! Let's face it: heterosexuality is still the favorite sex style of almost three billion adults on Planet Earth. A homosexual union is only more exciting *if you think it is*. This is one time the majority is right.

Of the two factors in becoming homosexual—a predisposition and a learned behavior—the learning process is by far the more important. It is even possible to skip the predisposition in the formula and still produce a homosexual. Again, a predisposition toward homosexuality does not a homosexual make. Only if an individual allows his predisposition to inspire homosexual thoughts so that he moves in a same-sex direction will he become homosexual. He must then commit a homosexual act, find pleasure in it, and think favorably toward it (or learn to), perpetuating such acts and such thoughts exclusively until all his sexual feelings are directed to persons of his own sex. And contrary to popular homosexual teachings, such feelings, thoughts, and actions are reversible!

Learning through Loneliness

Loneliness is rapidly becoming the most chronic emotional problem of this nuclear age. Until you have felt the cold, numbing sense of isolation that fills many people's hearts

when their natural desire for companionship goes unfulfilled,
you aren't capable of assessing how powerful a force it is.
Counselors have long known that many women have traded
heterosexual sex for companionship even back in the days
when pregnancy was almost certain to follow. Now we are
recognizing that it is the natural craving for another, a reaching
for and the sharing of intimate experiences, that make lesbians
and homosexuals out of young people who really had no
predisposition toward homosexuality. It is quite common for
homosexuals to deny that they "recruit" young people into
homosexuality, but in actuality many are brought into it that
way. In particular, the lonely boy or girl without any
predisposition toward homosexuality may be willing to
tolerate even distasteful sex in order to gain companionship.
Homosexuals call such people "chickens," and they bestow
the uncomplimentary title of "chicken hawk" upon those who
seek them out and through the offer of "love" entice them into
their homosexual bed.

Such liaisons may last a week, a year, or longer, but usually
by the time they break up, the former "chicken" has
developed a mental pattern of thinking same-sex thoughts
and thus has created same-sex feelings and appetites. The
first "chicken hawk" has not only created a homosexual but
bred another "chicken hawk." In fairness to homosexuals,
they may never have set out deliberately to pervert the sexual
direction of a young person. But it happened, nevertheless.
Probably they too were driven by an intense loneliness to share
their life (for a time) with another. But sooner or later the
perverted sex drive cries out for expression, and they recruit
another chicken for the movement.

Gradually the tempo increases. The first liaison may last
several months or years (as they like to describe it: "I lived
with my first 'lover' for three years.") But usually subsequent
encounters (particularly with men) are less enduring. Only
God knows how many "chickens" one "hawk" can entice

into homosexuality in a lifetime. But since it is impossible for homosexuals to propagate, they must recruit to enjoy companionship, sex, or both.

Tragically, this recruiting usually takes place at the time young people should be thinking about marriage, family, and intimate companionship with the opposite sex. However, when they are recruited to homosexuality under the guise of a "gay life style," they become victims of what I consider the world's cruelest hoax. As we have already observed, "Gay it isn't." One reason for this book is to save innocent "chickens" from becoming "hawks." Another is to tell them the good news—there is a way out!

CHAPTER FIVE

Is
There
a Cure?

"Once Gay Always Gay" is an
increasingly familiar cry in the homosexual community. This
is a deceitful maxim, but its popularity among the homosexual
crowd and their readiness to engage in militant verbal combat
on the subject indicate its pervasiveness. A prominent Los
Angeles psychiatrist reports, "In all my years of counseling, I
have never cured a homosexual, and I don't know of any other
psychiatrist who has, either."

This pessimistic appraisal may be somewhat exaggerated,
but not excessively so. For the truth is, homosexuality is one
of the most difficult habits of life to overcome, and few
secular counselors report any viable success. In the early
1970s a famous psychiatrist published a book verifying that
his therapy had been effective in reversing the sex direction of
over 30 percent of the homosexuals he treated. Two years ago
another psychiatrist discounted all those so-called "changes."
The latter psychiatrist claimed to have visited his nationally
known colleague and asked to interview some of the "cured"
patients. None could be produced!

In talking to psychiatrists, psychologists, and other
counselors, I have asked two questions: 1) Have you seen any
homosexuals change the direction of their sex drive and make

a satisfactory conversion to a heterosexual life? 2) Do you
know of any other counselors who have? To both questions I
have received consistently negative answers.

Most homosexuals do not seek a counselor because they
desire to change. Those I have counseled come in because of
depression after being jilted by a "lover" or because they are
in trouble with parents, wife, boss, or society. Few
homosexuals want to change their sexual direction. They
would prefer that society accept them as they are.

For many decades, the answer of psychotherapy to this
dilemma has been, "You have a deep-rooted psychological
problem. You need a battery of psychological tests and a long
series of counseling encounters or psychoanalysis." Very
frankly, only a small percent of the population can afford
such treatment, and even then success is questionable. Group
therapy is cheaper and more popular today, but reports I hear
indicate that it is more apt to entrench individuals in their
homosexuality than to free them.

Another futile attempt at curing the problem is the
transference method. The client is taught to transfer his
homosexual thoughts to heterosexual thoughts. A
reinforcement process uses a series of homosexual and
heterosexual slides. Each time a homosexual slide is flashed
on the screen, an electric impulse generates a resounding
shock, intended to make homosexual images undesirable and
force the individual to enjoy heterosexual thoughts. Then
provocative nude opposite-sex slides appear on the screen.
The next step is for the person to experience successful
opposite-sex experience, perhaps even with a prostitute. If the
costly process works (which is debatable), what really has
happened is that the permissive homosexual is changed into a
permissive fornicator.

So far I've given you the bad news. Now let's take a look at
the good news.

There Is a Cure
for Homosexuality!

What would you think if I told you that I know a man who was homosexual for thirty-seven years and is now happily straight? Or a thirty-five-year-old woman who claimed to have "same-sex impulses for as far back as I can remember," but has been straight for five years? Today she ministers to many lesbians in her area and is planning to marry a former homosexual, who has been helping men step out of the unhappy gay life into a blessed new experience. Would you like to believe the story of the married minister and father of two children whose nightly escapades kept him out until 3 A.M. for the worst part of seven years, but who is now so changed that he helps to deliver others from homosexuality? I know of doctors, school teachers, musicians, and artists who were unhappy gays but now are "new" people. Some dragged their family through the torment of withdrawal from the un-gay life; others slipped out of it quietly. But there is such a growing number of these former homosexuals that they hold their own annual convention. Many who attend return to their own communities to counsel others out of this increasingly popular but privately unhappy life style.

In talking to "former gays," as they call themselves, or in listening to their cassette tapes designed to help others, I find three common denominators in each exit story:

1. It is not easy to come out of homosexuality.
2. The individual really has to want to change his life style.
3. No one can do it alone! It takes external help to successfully forsake homosexuality.

Needed:
A Changed Nature

Homosexuals are right about one thing: it is their nature to

be homosexual. They were lured gradually, as we have seen,
from thought to feeling to experience, which increased the
thoughts and feelings and led to more experiences until
homosexuality became an entrenched part of their nature. The
only way they will ever reverse the process is to undergo a
change of nature. For that they need outside help, which is
exactly what Jesus Christ came to give them. The Bible
teaches that when a person receives Christ, he becomes "a
partner of the divine nature, having escaped the corruption
that is in the world through lust" (2 Peter 1:4). That divine
(or new) nature in Christ is the external reality that has enabled
every ex-homosexual I know or have heard of to make his exit
and assume a normal life. As already stated, it isn't easy,
particularly for those who have lived a homosexual life for
many years, but it is possible.

When Jesus Christ enters a person's life, he imparts to him
a new set of desires and feelings. The things he once loved he
gradually grows to hate, and many of the things he previously
hated he begins to love. One lesbian shared with me that she
had never desired to marry a man, for she had curried the favor
only of women. Now that she had forsaken her lesbian way of
life, she had met a man she admired, become his friend, and
now seriously contemplated marriage. Not all homosexuals
who receive Jesus Christ as Lord and Savior become
heterosexual to the point of marriage, but all can be
transformed.

When invited into a person's life, Jesus Christ gives him the
power to become a child of God (John 1:12). That means he
is spiritually adopted as one of God's children, which solves
the alienation-from-God feeling that homosexuals so often
have. In fact, Jesus Christ resolves many problems for a
homosexual, just as he does for any other lost soul.

1. Christ pardons him from all sin. "But if we walk in the
light, as he is in the light, we have fellowship one with
another, and the blood of Jesus Christ his Son cleanseth us
from all sin . . . If we confess our sins, he is faithful and just

to forgive us our sins, and to cleanse us from all
unrighteousness" (1 John 1:7, 9). Every person needs
forgiveness for his sin of rebellion against God and for his
self-will, which causes him to disobey God.

2. He gives peace with God (Romans 5:1): "Therefore
being justified by faith, we have peace with God through our
Lord Jesus Christ." The peace in the life of a homosexual is
twofold. The first phase is "peace with God," which fills
that vacuum formed by his enmity toward God. The second
is a gradual subsiding of the intense hostility that seems
to characterize his interpersonal relationships. As one
of the first evidences that a homosexual has received Christ,
he is easier to get along with and that fire of anger within him
begins to die.

3. Christ makes him a new creature. "Therefore if any man
be in Christ, he is a new creature; old things are passed away;
behold all things are become new" (2 Corinthians 5:17).
Gradually this new creature will discontinue his homosexual
life style. Many former homosexuals testify that they tried
several times to break their homosexual habits but failed until
they became Christians. Then the power of the "new nature,"
created in them by God when they received Christ, enabled
them to successfully break this habit.

4. He gives him a new joy in life. "And not only so, but we
also joy in God through our Lord Jesus Christ, by whom we
have now received the atonement" (Romans 5:11). All writers
on homosexuality agree that every homosexual experiences an
enormous amount of loneliness and despair. When he receives
Christ, he "joys in God," that is, he forms a liaison with a
new friend who is always with him to supply the fellowship
and companionship his heart has yearned for. That is what
Jesus Christ meant when he said, "Behold, I stand at the door
and knock: if any man hear my voice, and open the door, I will
come in to him, and will sup with him, and he with me"
(Revelation 3:20).

Homosexuals are not the only ones who need that constant

companionship with Jesus Christ. Every human being should personally invite him into his life as Lord and Savior so that he can have his sins forgiven, enjoy peace with God, become a new creature, and be assured of the constant companionship of Jesus Christ.

5. God gives him eternal life, "Verily, verily, I say unto you, he that heareth my word, and believeth on him that sent me, hath everlasting life, and shall not come into condemnation; but is passed from death unto life" (John 5:24).

Most sinners, and particularly homosexuals, have a hard time accepting the fact that they can *really* possess eternal life. Although all of us intuitively want it, we tend to feel that we do not deserve it, and we are prone to deem it an insubstantial ideal. Fortunately, our feelings have nothing to do with it. Eternal life is an undeserved gift which God dispenses to man, not because he deserves it, but because God loves him and in his mercy has chosen to impart it through faith in his Son Jesus Christ.

Self-will or God's Will

We live in a day when the term "born-again Christian" has become so popular that it is recognized from prison to the White House, but it is questionable whether all those who know the term understand the experience. The most misunderstood part of being born again is the exchange of wills—that is, turning from self-will to God's will.

A self-willed person can do anything he wants with his life, mentally, socially, vocationally, and even sexually. A truly born-again Christian, however, has not only confessed his sin to God in order to gain forgiveness but is willing to do God's will instead of his own. That is what the Bible means when it speaks of calling on the *Lord* Jesus Christ, or believing on

the *Lord* Jesus Christ to be saved. Asking Christ to become
Lord of your life means that you are eager to do *his* will, not
your own. The will of God on basic issues is not difficult to
discern, for it is taught clearly in his Word. For example, the
Bible says, "Thou shalt not steal." When a thief is converted,
not only his spiritual life but his vocational life is changed.
He stops stealing. The same can be said for adultery. Because
the Bible teaches, "Thou shalt not commit adultery," a
converted adulterer will stop this heinous practice.

In this connection Jesus Christ made an awesome
announcement in his Sermon on the Mount (Matthew 7:21-23):

> Not every one that saith unto me, Lord,
> Lord, shall enter into the kingdom of
> heaven; but he that doeth the will of my
> Father which is in heaven.
>
> Many will say to me in that day, Lord,
> Lord, have we not prophesied in thy name?
> and in thy name have cast out devils? and
> in thy name done many wonderful works?
>
> And then will I profess unto them, I
> never knew you: depart from me, ye that
> work iniquity.

This passage and many others clearly teach that a truly
"born-again Christian" does not pursue his own will but that
of God, as revealed in the Bible. That is not to say he never
sins; in fact, he will, occasionally. But provision has been
made for such sin (1 John 2:1, 2 and 1:9), and when confession
follows transgression, the believer is again cleansed of that
sin. Basically he purposes to fulfill the will of God, not his
own will. That is really what "repentance" is all about. The
conversion from self-will to God's will opens the only avenue
of freedom from the captivity of homosexuality—or from
anything else that displeases God.

The only successful method of helping homosexuals out of
their unhappy way of life is for them to have this "born
again" experience. Only then will the power of God be

unleashed in their life, enabling them to "come out." It isn't easy, but it can be done!

A case in point is found in 1 Corinthians 6:9-11, where Paul praised the Corinthians for the transformation that occurred in their lives after they received Christ. After substantiating that fornicators, adulterers, homosexuals, and abusers of themselves with mankind will not enter the kingdom of heaven, he added, "And such *were* some of you; but [now] you are washed . . . sanctified . . . justified in the name of the Lord Jesus, and by the Spirit of our God." Obviously, then, some of the first Christians of the Corinthian church were saved out of extremely immoral life styles, including homosexuality. As incredible as it may seem, many of the founders of early Christianity in Europe were *former* homosexuals and adulterers, for as we have seen, homosexuality was a way of life in Greece. But they were delivered from that life style, an escape that God offers to men and women today. Jesus Christ is still in the life-changing business.

A Special Note

I would like to ask you a very important question. Have you *personally* invited Jesus Christ into your life as Lord and Savior? Whether homosexual or heterosexual, you need to if you have not already done so. Jesus said, "Except a man be born again, he cannot see the kingdom of heaven" (John 3:3).

If you would like to receive him today, just bow your head and utter a prayer like this: "Lord Jesus, I admit that I am a sinner; I need your forgiveness and cleansing. Come into my life and make me a new person. I really want to be your servant and do your will."

The Bible promises, "Whosoever shall call upon the name

of the Lord shall be saved'' (Romans 10:13). Thank him by faith for making you his child, find a Bible-believing church where you can study the Word of God, and share with the people there that you have received Christ. They will instruct you on Bible baptism as an open confession of your faith and show you how to read the Bible regularly for yourself.*

*To assist you in spiritual growth—new and young Christians are encouraged to secure a copy of the author's book, *How to Study the Bible for Yourself,* from your Christian bookstore, or you may order it from Family Life Seminars, 2100 Greenfield Drive, El Cajon, California 92021.

The Truth about Homosexuality

No one is prepared to deal adequately with homosexuality, either his own or another's, until he understands what it is. Many suggestions are offered today, most of which are erroneous. Some would have us believe it is a "quirk of nature." Others call it an "optional life style" as if it were a desirable choice. Some label it "mental or emotional illness" or "sickness." Still others would have us believe it is a "gift of God." All of these answers are seriously in error.

Next to self-preservation, the desire for sex is one of mankind's most basic drives. This in itself is not bad. As my wife and I describe in our book *The Act of Marriage*, sexual intercourse between husband and wife is life's most exciting, fulfilling, and uniting experience. It was designed by God for both pleasure and propagation. When God created Adam, he purposely shaped his maleness, including his sexual capabilities. When he made an ideal companion for man to fulfill his life's destiny and potential, he designed woman, including her femininity. There are many unique differences between them physically, mentally, and emotionally, but the easiest to identify is their sexuality. Throughout the Bible God's plan is announced clearly: one man and one woman "as long as they both shall live." Their sexual union was designed in part to cement their total union and to produce a "helpmate" relationship for them.

Right from the beginning, the deceiver of men (Satan) encouraged the violation of the sex drive in this order: adultery, homosexuality, incest, rape, bestiality, and prostitution. All of these sexual expressions were forbidden by God, and those who took pleasure in them in Old Testament days were sentenced to death. Such practices directly violated the will and plan of God for man because they inflicted irreparable damage upon the human race.

We should particularly note that whenever man turns away from God to worship idols, he also abuses his sex drive. Wherever you find false religion today, you encounter perversion of the sex drive through advocation of adultery, homosexuality, polygamy, celibacy, and in some cases voluntary or forcible castration. The misuse of the sex drive leads man away from God, and false concepts of God lead to the misuse of the sex drive. This is evidenced by the interchangeable use of the term "harlot" to mean both spiritual and physical fornicators. One leads to the other.

The culture of New Testament times was largely Grecian. Maimonides, a famous student of Greek history, maintained that men dressed in women's fancy clothes often came to worship Ashtoreth, while women came dressed in soldiers' armor. This was a B.C. attempt to religiously wipe out the distinction between men and women. It is not uncommon for idolatrous religions to confuse the sex roles of their gods, so it is only natural that their worshipers confuse their own.

The Bible not only condemns the illegitimate use of sex (including same-sex) but prohibits the wearing of clothes of the opposite sex. Deuteronomy 22:5 states, "The woman shall not wear that which pertaineth unto a man, neither shall a man put on a woman's garment; for all that do so are abomination unto the Lord thy God." Wearing clothing of the opposite sex

is an "abomination to God" because such an act tends to rub
out the lines of distinction between man and woman. A man
dressed in women's clothes tends to be effeminate, not
masculine, and a woman dressed like a man takes on coarse
mannerisms and tends to lose her femininity.

Homosexuality
Is Still a Sin!

Homosexuality is one of six sexual sins condemned by God
in the Old Testament, and nothing in the New Testament
changed that condemnation. Sometimes Christians are guilty
of making it appear as a grosser sin than others; that is false.
But it is still a sin God calls an "abomination" (Leviticus
18:22), and homosexuals must see it in that light or remain
incurable.

Almost everyone is aware that the Old Testament not only
considered homosexuality a sin but found it a capital offense,
that is, punishable by death. "If a man also lie with mankind,
as he lieth with a woman, both of them have committed an
abomination; they shall surely be put to death; their blood
shall be upon them" (Leviticus 20:13). This may seem "cruel
and inhuman treatment" by today's standards, but our
leniency has caused today's widespread problems. This is not
to suggest that Christians advocate the death penalty for
today's homosexuals, but I do have a question that needs
consideration. Who is *really* being cruel and inhuman—those
whose leniency allows homosexuality to spread to millions of
victims who would not otherwise have been enticed into this
sad and lonely life style, or those who practiced Old Testament
capital punishment?

Some in the homosexual church (which will be dealt with
in another chapter) would have us believe that the Old
Testament condemnations were negated through Christ and
that we are no longer under the Law. Obviously they are

unaware of the clear teachings of the New Testament on this matter, because the only thing that has changed is the death penalty. The New Testament condemns the practice even more harshly but lists the end as spiritual rather than physical death. 1 Corinthians 6:9, 10 says, "... no effeminate, nor abusers of themselves with mankind ... shall inherit the Kingdom of God." According to scholars, these Greek words, *malakoi* and *arsenokoitai*, mean "soft, effeminate persons ... such as catamites, men and boys who allow themselves to be misused homosexually," and "male homosexuals, pederasts, and sodomites." No competent Greek scholar would suggest that these mean anything but modern-day homosexuals.

In 1 Timothy Paul stated that the law was not made for righteous men, "but for the lawless and disobedient, for the ungodly and for sinners, for unholy and profane, for murderers of fathers and murderers of mothers, for manslayers, for fornicators, for *arsenokoitai* [homosexuals]." All of these, according to Paul, are "contrary to sound doctrine" (1 Timothy 1:9, 10).

The New Testament book that homosexuals hate more than any other, the one they continually seek to avoid, is Romans, for in chapter 1 their sexual preference is clearly condemned. In speaking of those who turned their backs on God to worship idols, Paul says, "God gave them up to uncleanness through the lusts of their own hearts to dishonor their own bodies between themselves" (Romans 1:24).

God's Description of Homosexuality

To help the reader better understand God's view of homosexuality in Romans 1:18-28, I list below his description:

Verse 18 Ungodliness
Unrighteousness
Hold the truth of God in unrighteousness

Verse 24 Uncleanness
          Dishonor their own body

Verse 26 Vile affections
          Against nature (women with women)

Verse 27 Burned in their lust
          That which is shameful (men with men)

Verse 29 Reprobate mind

By no stretch of the imagination can anyone be helped or improved in life by adopting a homosexual life style. Clearly it is ungodly, vile, against nature, and shameful. It leads inevitably to a "reprobate mind," that is, a mind with a conscious bent toward sinning. The text certainly explains the arrogant, open defiance that characterizes many of the leaders of today's militant homosexual movement—they have a reprobate mind. Add to that the basic anger that characterizes all homosexuals, plus their obsessive selfishness, and you begin to understand why they are so driven to make their depraved life style widely accepted. Homosexuality is certainly not the only sin, and everyone should consider this sinful life style in the light that he too is a sinner. Perhaps this life style incurs the wrath of God in such a severe way because more than any other sin, it tends to pervert most people who adopt it. Even though adultery, incest, prostitution, and even bestiality are capital offenses condemned by God, they do not usually destroy the man-woman potential of the individual the way homosexuality does. While some homosexuals claim to be bisexual, most are exclusively same-sex oriented. Certainly no sexual practice is so destructive of an entire society as homosexuality; the other sins mentioned do not seem to involve the intense sexual obsessions that are usually associated with homosexuality.

The first known report of homosexuality in all of history is a case in point. You are probably familiar with the story of

Sodom and Gomorrah found in Genesis 19 (where we get the time-honored word for homosexual practice, "sodomy"). Two angelic messengers of God came to visit Lot, but before they settled in for the night, men of Sodom surrounded the house and demanded he send his guests out to them so they might sexually "know" them. Even Lot's cowardly attempt to barter his two virgin daughters for the safety of his guests was refused, for they were so perverted that they had no interest in women. When the Sodomites tried to break down the door, the angels "smote them with blindness, both small and great." But these men were so sexually obsessed that even in their blindness "they wearied themselves to find the door."

The homosexual church theologians' suggestion that Sodom's sin was really "lack of hospitality" rather than immorality is not only ridiculous, it is unscholarly. Why would inhospitality make them so lust crazy as to seek the door after being blinded? Only a sexually degenerate obsession like homosexuality could so fan their lustful passions.

It is no wonder that God destroyed Sodom with fire and brimstone, for the citizens were "perverted," "reprobate in mind," "given to vile affections," "obsessed with an 'unnatural' sex direction" and "ungodly." Some Bible scholars teach that homosexuality is the ultimate sin of man's abominations and that when it is rampant in a society, God destroys that society. Whether the many homosexual civilizations no longer in existence destroyed themselves or whether God destroyed them as he did Sodom, I am not prepared to say. But upon viewing the brimstone at the south end of the Dead Sea that covers the ruins of Sodom, and after tramping around the ruins of Pompeii, Rome, and Athens, I saw sufficient signs of homosexuality to make me wonder if the rapid decline of Great Britain should not be attributed to the 1957 legalization of homosexuality. Not one major nation today has so dignified this sin against man and God (including communist Russia, which prohibits sodomy), though many of the weak and dependent nations have legalized it. God have mercy on America if we ever officially endorse this "shameful" sin against nature!

Can a Christian Be a Homosexual?

Homosexuality is not just a sin against one's own body, but an offense against God. Therefore the phrase "a Christian homosexual" is really a contradiction of terms. A homosexual violates God's clearly prescribed will, thwarts his purpose for man, and has incurred "the wrath of God." If a man persists in this sin long enough, God will "give him up to a reprobate mind."

Our married son gave a ride to a hitchhiker approximately his age and tried to share Christ with him. Finding that Larry is a Christian, the emotionally upset lad rehearsed the stormy session he had just experienced with his parents, who were active Christians in a leading church in our city but were not prepared to handle their son's announcement, "I'm a gay Christian." His father had angrily ordered him out of the house, thundering, "I never want to see you again until you straighten out your life." The heartbroken young man lamented, "My parents just can't believe I can be a Spirit-filled Christian homosexual." Neither can God! For a Spirit-filled Christian is a Spirit-controlled person, one who will do those things that please God as he reveals himself in his Word. You can be sure of this—a truly Spirit-controlled Christian will never be led into homosexuality by the Holy Spirit.

This young man had three problems. First, his parents reacted in anger rather than in love, thus compounding the problem. Second, he attended the homosexual church in our community where an ordained homosexual minister in clerical garb taught him that "gay is just as good as straight" and, contrary to God's Word, "gay is beautiful." Finally, if he really is a Christian, he will ultimately commit the "sin unto death" (1 John 5:16)—that is, physical death as a result of protracted willfulness and disobedience.

Although a Christian cannot be a committed homosexual, a former homosexual may stumble into a homosexual sin occasionally. In fact, several of the former homosexuals who now are successfully carrying on a ministry to homosexuals admit that as baby Christians they stumbled. Everyone who knows anything about homosexuality has to admit that it is usually very difficult to extricate a person from this life style. As we saw in the last chapter, by the power of Jesus Christ it is possible, and many today are conquering the habit, but anyone who says it is easy is either kidding himself or doesn't know what he is talking about. Sometimes a person will have instantaneous deliverance from this sin and its temptation, but I have found such cases extremely rare.

Let's face it: no Christian is perfect. I have never met a former adulterer, liar, thief, or egomaniac who didn't sin occasionally after he became a Christian. But God has made ample provision for us in 1 John 1:7-9 to repent, gain forgiveness, and be reinstated by his grace and mercy. Were it not for this renewing experience, none of us would make it. Satan knows our "besetting sin" and usually tempts us where we are weakest. You can be sure he will work on a former homosexual's sin the same way. However, if the young convert confesses his sin, he too can be forgiven. There is no end to the grace of God for the sincere soul. The only time a homosexual has cause to fear the wrath of God is when he rebelliously, stubbornly, and persistently clings to this perverted life style. Such souls vainly (but loudly) seek to justify their actions. They are dangerous because they are carriers of infection. All such cases with which I am familiar eventually came to an untimely and tragic end.

Homosexuality: An Eternally Fatal Sin

Recently a man waited to see me after a church service. His first statement was, "I understand you are writing a book for homosexuals to be called *The Unhappy Gays*." Then he proudly said, "I want you to meet a happy one." He also insisted he was a "born-again Christian." I responded, "You're kidding yourself on both counts." A Christian homosexual will either be trying to extricate himself from his sin or will feel so guilty about it he is miserable. A Christian is one who basically seeks to obey the Word of God. A homosexual is deceiving himself if he thinks he can practice that life style and still go to Heaven. On that, the Scripture is extremely clear. Consider the following three passages. In Romans 1:27-32 the men, "leaving the natural use of the woman, burned in their lust one toward another, men with men working that which is unseemly . . without natural affection . . who, knowing the judgment of God, that they who commit such things are worthy of death. . . ." The death Paul has in mind is spiritual death or eternal damnation. In 1 Corinthians 6:9, 10 he asks, "Know ye not that the unrighteous shall not inherit the kingdom of God? *Be not deceived*; neither fornicators, nor idolaters, nor adulterers, nor effeminate, nor abusers of themselves with mankind . . shall inherit the kingdom of God." Since the word "effeminate" in the Greek means homosexual, the obvious teaching of this text is that anyone who makes adultery, fornication, idolatry, or homosexuality a way of life will not inherit eternal life.

A third text that makes the eternal end of the homosexual quite clear is Jude 7. God tells us that "Sodom and Gomorrah, and the cities about them" that gave themselves over to "fornication and going after strange flesh, are set forth for an

example, suffering the vengeance of eternal fire." Such
tragic terms as "deserving of death," "eternal fire," and
"shall not inherit eternal life" stand as graphic warnings to
anyone who will objectively examine the Word of God. There
is no question—a person who practices homosexuality as a
way of life cannot be a Christian.

Judge Not Lest Ye Be Judged

If there was ever a time when a man or woman needs true
Christian love, it is when he is trying desperately to "come
out" of homosexuality because he has become a Christian.
Jesus did not condemn Peter after a threefold denial; he just
looked at him. After his resurrection, our Lord went to Peter
to assure him of his love. I have found that homosexuals have
an enormous need for that kind of forgiving love. Don't
condemn the Christian brother when he falls. Help to lift him
back up. Your wholesome companionship may be one of the
tools God uses to give victory over this perverted life style.
The Holy Spirit will convict him. He doesn't need your
condemnation; he needs you. Almost all homosexuals require
a close straight friend in order to leave that life style.

A homosexual whom I counseled several times (and who
today is a victorious Christian) confessed his sin immediately
at the beginning of each interview. If he had fallen into sin
between sessions, his guilt was so intense that he felt I could
see it on his face (actually I couldn't, but he thought so). The
fact that I would pray with him reassured him that God would
forgive him. Gradually he found complete deliverance.

The true Christian attitude should be the same as our Lord's
—he hated the sin but loved the sinner. Remember the
adulteress brought to him for stoning? He said, "Neither do
I condemn thee; go and sin no more" (John 8:11). If he were

here in the flesh today, that would be his response to the
repentant homosexual: "Thy sins be forgiven thee—go and
sin no more." But be sure of this: Christ would insist that we
recognize the truth about homosexuality. It is a sin.

Homosexual Feelings Are Not Sin

Christians need to be understanding of the person whose
predisposition toward homosexuality occasionally sparks
homosexual feelings. It is unrealistic to suggest that such
urgings do not exist. And it is cruel and inhuman treatment
to dump a load of unnecessary guilt on people for having
such feelings. That spontaneous response is not sin. Only lurid
fantasies and prolonged same-sex desires would constitute a
sinful thought pattern. You cannot always control what
thoughts enter your mind, but you can determine how long
they remain.

   This study of homosexuality should enable you to
distinguish between homosexuals and those who have
homosexual feelings. We in the church must be careful in
condemning homosexuality as sin, for we commonly create
guilt in the person who is struggling with homosexual
feelings. Such individuals, of course, must recognize these
feelings as dangerous to him, as is lust to the heterosexual.
Just as most men wage a lifetime battle against adulterous
thoughts so as not to violate our Lord's command not to "lust
after a woman," so those with homosexual feelings must
guard their minds and hearts daily or they will never develop
the "pure mind" we are taught in Scripture to seek. Such
individuals should understand that homosexual feelings are
not sin, but even momentary contemplation of them makes
that person vulnerable. He or she should be extremely careful

to cast down evil imaginations and bring "into captivity every thought to the obedience of Christ" (2 Corinthians 10:5).

Homosexuality Is a Sin Against the Body

The Bible places sexual sins in a special category, calling them "sins against the body." These include all heterosexual violations of the laws of God as well as homosexual sins. Then the Scripture points out that such sins are extremely harmful, for they keep us from being "joined unto the Lord." The Christian's body does not belong to him—it is the Lord's. Ponder this Bible passage carefully:

> Flee fornication. Every sin that a man doeth is without the body; but he that committeth fornication sinneth against his own body. What? know ye not that your body is the temple of the Holy Spirit which is in you, which ye have of God, and ye are not your own? For ye are bought with a price. Therefore glorify God in your body, and in your spirit, which are God's (1 Corinthians 6:18-20).

CHAPTER SEVEN

How to Overcome Homosexuality

No sin is easy to overcome. The more it is indulged, the more deeply entrenched the habit becomes—and that is exactly what a long-practiced sin is, a sinful habit. The deeper the habit, the harder it will be to overcome, no matter what its nature. This is probably why some psychiatrists report that the only homosexuals they have seen changed are "young people." One even went so far as to say, "If they have been practicing homosexuality for ten years and are over thirty, it is irreversible." That statement is not true for Christians. But it does verify that the longer a habit has been practiced, the harder it will be to overcome. Yet I have heard the testimonies of former homosexuals who claim deliverance through Christ after enslavements of over twenty or, in one case, thirty-seven years.

In fairness to homosexuals, we must face the fact that their sin is extremely difficult to conquer—but so are other sins. Years ago I made the mistake of treating homosexuals as if their sin habit were the hardest of all to break. Since then I have found that nymphomania (the perversion of a woman driven by insecurity to promiscuous sex) is equally difficult to overcome, as are breaking off an adulterous "affair" with a partner you deeply "love," kleptomania, lying, alcoholism, drug addiction, and self-pity on the part of the deeply depressed. Actually, I have found that whatever sin habit is destroying a person's life, to him it is the most difficult sin in the world to gain victory over. Why? Because his childhood and temperament have probably given him a predisposition toward it, and a lifetime of habit has ingrained it in his nature until it seems as natural as breathing.

Why, then, should a homosexual, adulterer, alcoholic, or any other sinner want to rid himself of that one compulsive habit that brings supreme pleasure to his life? Because he doesn't like it? Not at all. Those who have "come out" of homosexuality have done so because they detest the shame, guilt, rejection, loneliness, and estrangement from God that follows in the wake of their sin. The same is true for any other sinner. Of the many people I have counseled, few have sought spiritual advice in order to overcome their sin. Most come because they can't handle the negative feelings caused by their sin. Frankly, not all of them have been willing to change their life style to gain the relief they crave. But I have learned that one principle is basic: you cannot violate the laws of God and attain lasting happiness. Jesus Christ said, "Blessed are they that hear the Word of God and *keep* it" (Luke 11:28). I have discovered that miserable people have earned the right to be miserable and will find help *only* when they are willing to let God turn their lives from disobedience to his will to full obedience. Only an act of faith and an assertion of the will brings about such a transformation.

An important note: All counselors of homosexuals agree upon one precept: whether a Christian or non-Christian, a homosexual cannot be helped unless *he really wants help.* Bill Gothard once said, "You cannot help a person unless he is desperate," and that is true! Those who come to me after losing a "lover" are usually bad risks unless they receive Christ and recognize their homosexuality as exceedingly sinful. Oftentimes they visit a counselor out of despair due to rejection and loneliness. Consequently, if they do not realize the blind alley their life style will lead them into and face the sin involved, they will return to it as soon as the next "lover" comes along. Only by facing their transgressions as sinful, resulting in tragedy, heartache, and death (physically and spiritually), will they be willing to pay the price to come out of this life style. In all honesty, of course, breaking the habits of homosexuality will not guarantee that the individual will become heterosexual.

Eighteen Steps to Overcoming Homosexuality

Having acknowledged that breaking this habit is difficult, I do not wish to leave the reader with the impression it is impossible to break, for it isn't. Many have "come out" of homosexuality to lead productive lives, but in each case three ingredients guaranteed success: 1) they had a strong desire to "come out"; 2) they accepted the external power of God to help them; and 3) they gained support from other people i.e., family, friends, counselors, etc.). I know of no instance in which a homosexual licked his problem alone. Consider the following steps that have proven helpful to others:

One. Accept Jesus Christ as Savior and Lord. The first step toward victory is that personal experience with Jesus Christ which was detailed in chapter 5. Every sinner needs God's help in overcoming sin. Satan is a supernatural adversary who destroys men by getting them to capitulate to their most vulnerable weaknesses. To counteract his power, we need the supernatural, dynamic power of Jesus Christ, who is our "victory." As the Scripture says, "For we wrestle not against flesh and blood, but against . . . spiritual wickedness in high places" (Ephesians 6:12). Once you receive Christ, the spiritual power within will enable you to overcome Satan. Remember, "Greater is he that is in you than he that is in the world" (1 John 4:4).

Two. Be Continually Controlled by the Holy Spirit.

"And be not drunk with wine, wherein is excess; but be filled with the Spirit" (Ephesians 5:18).

A literal interpretation of that command of God could well read, "Be continually controlled by the Holy Spirit just as a drunk is continually controlled by alcohol." This requires a voluntary and continuous attitude of submission to the will of God as he reveals it in his Word. Whenever you find a spirit of resistance to the will of God, it is not the Spirit of God. Confess it and once again surrender your life in obedience to Christ. Christians who are continually controlled by his Holy Spirit do not commit homosexual acts (or other sins of the flesh).

Three. Walk in the Spirit.

"This I say then, Walk in the Spirit, and ye shall not fulfil the lust of the flesh" (Galatians 5:16).

Walking in the control of the Spirit is the practical implementation of the previous command that all Christians be continually controlled by the Spirit. The only way a Christian can overcome homosexuality or any other sinful habit is to be "strong in the Lord," and that comes from walking in the Spirit, which involves the following three ingredients:

> a. Read and obey the Word of God *daily*. Just as you need physical food to keep your body strong physically, you need daily spiritual food to preserve spiritual vitality. I have never known a dynamic Christian who did not regularly read, study, and memorize God's Word.
>
> b. Pray daily. One of the blessings of

the Christian life is that we are God's
children and have access to him through
prayer any time we need him. The Bible
continually challenges believers to
"pray without ceasing." Learn to talk
everything over with God until it
becomes a subconscious habit.

c. Confess all sin *immediately*. Yes, in
spite of your good intentions, you will
sin (hopefully, not with homosexual
acts, but doubtless you face other sinful
habits which, if practiced, will weaken
your spiritual life and make you
susceptible to your primary sin). Satan
will then rush to the attack and beat
you down with discouragement,
snarling, "See, you're not a good
Christian. You lied, cheated, etc." By
confessing your sin immediately, you
invoke 1 John 1:9 and are reinstated in
fellowship with God and the control
of his Spirit, thus defeating Satan and
reducing the effectiveness of his
temptations.

**Four.
Face
Homosexuality
As a *Sin* and
Confess It.**

All victory over sin starts with the
realization that it is wrong. For
example, one of the most successful
areas of counseling for me
personally has been in helping men
overcome the sin of anger. But I have never seen a man
overcome his hostility when he excused it and would not face
it as sin.

The same is true of homosexual sinners. Unless they are
willing to admit that *all* eight references to homosexuality
in Scripture (Genesis 19:1-11; Leviticus 18:22; 20:13;
Deuteronomy 23:17; Judges 19:22-25; Romans 1:26, 27;
1 Corinthians 6:9, 10; 1 Timothy 1:9, 10) condemn it as sinful
and call it unnatural or brand it a perversion, they will
never overcome it.

Whenever I hear a brainwashed victim of the Gay
Revolution, though a professing Christian, say,

"Homosexuality is not the worst sin in the world," or defend
it in some way, I groan within, for I know he is playing with
the fires of defeat. A truly repentant attitude toward sin was
reflected by the Apostle Paul, who thought of himself as "the
chief of sinners." What is the chief sin? Yours. When the
adulterer thinks his is "the greatest," I know he will be able
to erect impregnable defenses against Satan. For in his case
he is right—it is his chief sin. Until a homosexual admits
that his unnatural lust is sin, he is likely to experience many
dismal times of defeat. But if he confesses it to God as sin,
he not only enjoys forgiveness (1 John 1:9), but also the
Lord's power to overcome it. Confession of sin is the "giant
step" in overcoming homosexuality. Those who refuse to take
this step will never overcome it.

Five. Face and Confess Your Basic Anger Problem.

"And grieve not the Holy Spirit of
God, whereby ye are sealed unto the
day of redemption. Let all bitterness,
and wrath, and anger, and clamor,
and evil speaking be put away from
you, with all malice: And be ye kind
one to another, tenderhearted, forgiving one another, even as
God for Christ's sake hath forgiven you" (Ephesians
4:30-32).

Anger and homosexuality are inseparable sins. Every
counselor I know has detected the intense anger that churns
through even the most phlegmatic homosexual. Now that you
have studied the chapter on the cause of homosexuality, it
should be easy to understand why homosexuals are such angry
people. Probably the most psychologically destructive
experience a person can have in life is rejection, and
homosexuals understandably react to their multiple rejections
with anger.

Dr. William W. Halcomb, a family doctor, has been a close
Christian friend for a number of years. He spent many hours

sharing counseling concepts with me and helped immeasurably in formulating several of the concepts found in two of my books.* Years ago he learned the art of hypnosis to aid in delivering babies and later discovered it to be a helpful tool in counseling. His following encounter with a homosexual is a classic illustration of the anger that forms so basic a part of this problem.[27]

HOMOSEXUALITY—A CASE HISTORY
by William W. Halcomb, M.D.

When asked the question, "What seems to be your problem?" W. P. answered, "What it has always been, the homosexual problem. When I was fourteen I first started thinking about it and started masturbating. When I was eighteen I had my first voluntary homosexual experience. When I had mononucleosis, it was temporarily suppressed. About this time I started drinking and taking drugs. I was determined to try to put faith in Christ out of my mind so I stayed 'stoned' most of the time."

W. P. had already been under psychiatric care when he presented himself to my office. He had been to a psychiatrist about ten times without any encouragement or evidence there would be hope for his problem (homosexual behavior). This young man seemed to be sincerely interested in finding the solution for his problem so he was accepted as a patient for analysis to expose the origin of his homosexual behavior, and subsequently was treated for the same.

He had never had any heterosexual experiences but had had many girl friends whom he "loved" but never had any sexual desire for them. At the time he first came to me he was off all drugs except alcohol, which was still a problem. W. P.'s parents were separated during most of his childhood.

How to Be Happy Though Married and *How to Win over Depression.*

He remembered little of his father except that he was always kind to him. His father was overweight, had alcohol problems, and eventually stole money for alcohol. On the other hand, his mother worked constantly to support the children. He had always considered his mother the "rock" of the family. W.P.'s physical appearance is that of an intelligent, sincere young man, fair, very thin, and as he expressed it, had many of the same physical features as his mother. He got along well with his brother, ten years older than himself, but not with his sister. He had contemplated suicide many times, but actually tried it only once while a junior in high school.

Using hypnosis to facilitate the analysis, it was discovered that he had a complete denial of himself as a male. He was desirous of punishment because of his guilt. He harbored a tremendous resentment and hatred of his mother because she was always leaving him to go to work, or to go out on a date. Most important— his mother had tried to commit suicide and he was thereafter afraid she was going to die and leave him alone again. She had repeated such suicide attempts and taken trips to the hospital several times. W.P.'s word association test under hypnosis (which reveals the actual subconscious response to the words) is very interesting. (Dr.) "life" (W.P.) "death"—(Dr.) "hate" (W.P.) "death"—(Dr.) "penis" (W.P.) "hate"—(Dr.) "death" (W.P.) "life"—(Dr.) "anger" (W.P.) "hate"— (Dr.) "horrible" (W.P.) "death"—(Dr.) "resent" (W.P.) "mother"—(Dr.) "hostility" (W.P.) "anger"—(Dr.) "dominate" (W.P.) "submit"—(Dr.) "submit" (W.P.) "me"—(Dr.) "masturbate" (W.P.) "kill . . . my deepest thoughts tell me—I'm alive, at the bottom of it all—hate!"

There were several definite aspects to the

formation of homosexual behavior in this young man: (1) He was a very sensitive young boy who craved the attention and identity with a father which he did not have. (2) He sought love and affection from his mother, the "rock" and head of the home, which he did not get—but chose (subconsciously) to identify with her. Many people, including his mother, said that "we are just alike" in appearance and characteristics. (3) The tremendous desire to identify with his mother was precipitated at eight years of age. By putting on her underclothes he became sexually aroused, whereas his older sister's undergarments did not arouse him in any way. (4) Resentment, bitterness and hatred built up within him because his mother was always leaving him alone. She was either going out with men or going to the hospital. "Dying" implied her attempts at suicide or the many surgeries over a span of ten years. (5) By assuming the identity of his mother and her female traits he could compensate for his resentment and bitterness toward her for not giving the love and affection he craved in his younger years. W.P. stated, "I am like her and doing the same thing."
(6) By this same token he had to reject his own male characteristics; he reasoned it was better to be a homosexual than to have such strong emotions against his mother. Because this guilt was not due to any homosexual behavior but because of a fixed hatred toward his mother, he thus equated "death" and "hate" with his penis.
(7) This produced a tremendous desire for punishment plus denial of himself and his masculinity. After several counseling sessions W.P. concluded that the destructive emotion of *hate* was "at the bottom of it all."

Many boys, as they grow up, have various types of homosexual experiences and exposures, but that does not make them homosexuals! But with the stage set, W.P. was forced into a homosexual act when he was nine with his "big" cousin of fourteen. His cousin was also very kind to him, and dominant. Following this experience he indicated he "knew" he was "different" from the other boys in "every way."

Every converted homosexual wishing to extricate himself from this life style must come to grips with his anger. Usually it is directed toward his mother for rejecting, smothering, or dominating him. This often foments a hatred for women which makes heterosexuality all but impossible. Many a homosexual has tried to become sexually aroused by a woman but, in his failure to do so, mistakenly concluded he was incapable of male-female arousal. Actually, the culprit was anger at mother that spilled over to all women. Such a man may be able to carry on an amiable platonic relationship with women, much as he does with his mother, but it is as impossible for him to get aroused by a woman as for his mother to sexually stimulate him. Until this anger is removed, he will never manifest a normal emotional feeling for women.

As we have seen, the rejection of fathers can also arouse the anger that stifles normal love capabilities. The Bible sagely commands husbands to love their wives and "be not bitter against them" (Colossians 3:19). The reason is very simple: bitterness or anger destroys love. One cannot harbor bitterness and be loving at the same time!

Anger is a sin that grieves the Holy Spirit of God. Unless it is discontinued, it will prevent a Christian from being strong in the Lord, and in the case of homosexuals it will prohibit normal sexual love relationships.

The following steps for overcoming anger are taken from chapter 11 in my book *Understanding the Male*

Temperament,[28] where I deal more thoroughly with the
subject:

1. Face it as a sin; Ephesians 4:30-32.
2. Confess it; 1 John 1:9.
3. Ask God to take away the habit; 1 John 5:14, 15.
4. Ask forgiveness of the object of your wrath; James 5:16.
5. Thank God for the object of your wrath; 1 Thessalonians 5:18.
6. Ask God for the filling or control of his Spirit; Luke 11:13.
7. Repeat this formula each time you get angry.

**Six.
Love and
Accept Yourself.**
As in Dr. Halcomb's case history above, almost all homosexuals have a difficult time accepting themselves. This is also generally true of people with a Melancholic temperament. But if you add to that the heartbreak of childhood rejection and the social condemnation heaped upon homosexuals today, you can understand why they almost universally find it difficult to love, respect, and accept themselves. Jesus Christ taught that we are to love our neighbor as ourself. Obviously, then, a wholesome self-acceptance is necessary in life. It should never become narcissistic or obsessive to the point where we love ourselves more than God (Matthew 22:37-39), but the divine order is to love God first and then your neighbor as yourself.

Most self-rejecting homosexuals find little in themselves to like or love. They have been ridiculed so long by parents and peers that, being very sensitive by nature, they are certain nothing is right about them. A Christian should never think like that. Once forgiven of his sin by faith in Christ, he should thank God for who and what he is: "a son of God," "a joint heir with Jesus Christ," and an "heir of eternal life." As a

Christian, he is important to God and should consequently possess a strong self-image.

The best tool I have found for helping a person gain self-acceptance is the prayer of thanksgiving. That is, thank God for your looks, abilities, environment, and future in Christ. Replace all negative thoughts about yourself with praise and thanksgiving. As self-condemning thoughts gradually give way to thanksgiving, you will discover that you like yourself and the way God made you. The end result will be a victorious life used by God, which will assist your self-acceptance.

Seven.
Learn to Control
Your Mind.

"Casting down imaginations, and every high thing that exalteth itself against the knowledge of God, and bringing into captivity every thought to the obedience of Christ" (2 Corinthians 10:5).

Every sin-defeated Christian homosexual I have counseled admitted to evil fantasies prior to committing homosexual acts. The battle for control of the body is won or lost in the mind. It is not sufficient for such a Christian to vow, "I will never again commit homosexuality!" For if he indulges in homosexual lust thoughts, he will fan his emotions to such an intensity that he will be unable to control his sexual urges and will sin when an opportunity arises.

The human body is at the mercy of our emotions, for we are emotionally driven creatures. Man can control his natural emotions unless they are stimulated by his mind and imagination. It is interesting to note in this connection that the sex sins that precipitated the Flood in the days of Noah (some Bible scholars suggest that homosexuality was one of the sins) were the result of their "imaginations that were evil continually." Even today we find that those who practice abnormal sex in any of its expressions are usually into heavy pornography and X-rated movies. Such lust-producing

thoughts stimulate the emotions and cause passions that veer
out of control, generating actions that, when they are
consummated, produce sorrow, grief, and guilt. The time to
control them is when they begin in the mind.

Jesus Christ clarified the problem when he declared that
if a man lusts after a woman, he has committed heart adultery
(Matthew 5:28). Had he addressed himself to the homosexual,
I am confident he would have altered his statement to read,
"He that looketh at a man to lust after him has committed
homosexuality in his heart already." Such homosexual lustful
imaginations will lead to the "inordinate affections" or "vile
affections" that cause men to "burn in their lust one toward
another, men with men working that which is shameful"
(Romans 1:26, 27).

Victory over any sexual sin first enters the mind, then
infiltrates the body. Defeat follows the same route.
Homosexual thoughts lead to masturbation as one entertains
homosexual fantasies, which produces spiritual defeat. In the
succeeding spiritual depression, the homosexual is most
vulnerable to falling back into his old life style. Show me a
former homosexual who has gained victory, and I will
introduce you to a man or a woman who refuses to let his
imagination entertain suggestive, lurid homosexual thoughts
(or if he does, he confesses them immediately and replaces
those thoughts with the Word of God). As the Scriptures
teach, "Finally, brethren, whatever things are true . . . just
. . . pure . . . lovely . . . of good report, if there be any virtue,
and if there be any praise, *think on these things*" (Philippians
4:8).

Eight. Sincerely Thank God for Your Sexuality.

One step is often neglected in the
healing process of Christian
homosexuals: learning to accept and
appreciate their maleness or, in
the case of lesbians, their femininity.

We are sexually what we are by the design of God. He has not
made an error or perpetrated a cruel hoax on us by creating
us physically male and emotionally female. A God of love is
incapable of that kind of mistake or trickery. But almost all
homosexuals consciously or subconsciously reject their
sexuality. And if that carries over into their Christian
experience, it will definitely inhibit the extent of their healing.

Never underestimate the power of the mind. Someone has
said, "You are what you think you are." That is particularly
true of homosexuals. If you *think* you are "a woman trapped
in a man's body," you will *feel* like a woman, not a man. That
has nothing to do with your sexuality, but it has everything to
do with your mind, which produces the capacity to use your
sexuality. Some male homosexuals find it impossible to have
an erection in the presence of a woman (even though they may
love her as a person) because they think of themselves as a
woman sexually, in spite of their male genitals. If they change
their mind about their sexuality, they will gradually modify
their ability to respond to female stimuli.

Transsexuals provide a good illustration that the mind is
more powerful than the sex drive, determining the direction
it will take. Ever since Christine Jorgenson's operation,
changing her from male to female, misguided males have
sought to be made into women. A television documentary on
this subject recently indicated that 3,000 of these very
expensive operations are performed annually, and over
10,000 men have indicated their desire for "a sex change."
It would be much easier and less expensive to guide such
individuals to seek God's help in effecting a mental
transformation so they could function normally.
Unfortunately, the humanists who encourage such cruel and
inhuman treatment do not believe in God or the power of
Christ, so their best suggestion is to apply the surgeon's
scalpel to the genitals. What a tragic waste!

The latest research indicates that transsexuals have a low sex drive, are the passive recipients of the homosexual act, and develop a mental aversion to their genitalia to the point of hatred. This latter characteristic is illustrative of the power of the mind. A man wanting to be castrated is so repugnant and unnatural to the normal man that its very thought sends cold shivers down his spine. Why does a transsexual think like that? As a child he entertained the notion that he should have been a girl, and then the idea became a thought obsession until he looked on his own genitals as the one obstruction that stood in his path to becoming a woman. Therefore, what God meant to be a source of pleasure and fulfillment actually became his enemy—and all by the misuse of his mind.

Now let's reapply that mind power to the Christian we are trying to help come out of homosexuality. If he thinks he is a homosexual for life, he is! If he decides he can never respond to the opposite sex normally, he can't! Honest Christian counselors admit that not all their counselees who "come out of homosexuality" become heterosexual. Why is it that some, however, are able to marry and raise a Christian family, whereas others, even though they never return to the homosexual life style, are unable to become heterosexual? The mind! Either they never deal with the anger problem, or they do not learn to appreciate and thank God for their maleness or femaleness. In most cases they have not been counseled to develop a thankful spirit and a fresh appreciation for their sexuality as a gift from God.

Admittedly it is not easy to change a lifetime thinking pattern, but it can be accomplished by God's grace and power. What can be learned can be unlearned. And thinking of oneself as hopelessly caught in the snare of homosexuality limits the power of God. Those who have sought God's help in effecting a complete mental change testify it is worth the effort.

Nine. Make Absolutely No Exceptions.

Success in overcoming any habit, from the use of alcohol to eating fattening foods, is assured if the individual will follow one simple rule: *make absolutely no exceptions*. If the alcoholic never takes another drink, he has licked his problem. The same is true for the homosexual who repents of his sin and never again engages in a homosexual act. Take it from a "sweetaholic," it was easier to go three years without touching sweets than to make a few exceptions only to regain my old problem.

Ten. Avoid Homosexual Hangouts.

The Bible teaches us to "flee youthful lusts" and "avoid the very appearance of evil." The homosexual who continues to mix with his old homosexual friends or frequent the parks, restrooms, bars, beaches, or other places where they hang out is doomed to failure. The Bible teaches that "evil companions corrupt good morals" (1 Corinthians 15:33). A clean break with the old way of life and friends is essential to avoid temptation.

Some former homosexuals eventually become strong enough spiritually to revisit such places and friends, carrying a ministry to them. But even then it should be with a Christian companion. After all, our Lord sent his disciples out two by two. A wise Christian is aware of his own limitations. A homosexual will always be vulnerable to this form of temptation and should "make no allowance for the flesh to fulfill it in the lusts thereof."

Eleven. Become Active in a Bible-Teaching Church.

A good church is a haven for sinners. Most homosexuals think it only shelters "saints," but they fail to realize that a "saint" is "only a

sinner saved by grace.'' All of us in the church are former
sinners. We haven't all been homosexuals, but every one
of us seeks to overcome his own potential weakness from
which he has been saved, and the Bible teaches, ''There is
none righteous, no, not one!''

Unfortunately, some Christians react negatively when they
meet a former homosexual, primarily because they confuse
the sin and the sinner. In their opposition to homosexuality
they sometimes take out their animosity on those caught in
that life style. Gradually we in the church are maturing, and
an increasing number of believers are sharing their love and
understanding to the individual homosexual. Hopefully this
book will help speed that process. But even if the homosexual
is ''turned off'' at first (and he must not allow his naturally
sensitive nature to read more rejection into actions than really
exists), he does need a church home.

The Bible teaches, ''Forsake not the assembling of
yourselves together, as the manner of some is . . .'' (Hebrews
10:25). Homosexuals need the fellowship of other Christians
on a regular basis. They must hear the Word of God taught in
order to grow in their spiritual lives. They also need to know
divine principles for living. Most good churches feature both
Sunday morning and evening services, Sunday Bible study or
Sunday school, and Wednesday night Bible study and prayer
meeting. They should find a church where they feel the people
really enjoy studying the Word of God and love one another.
If they attend every time the doors are open, gradually they
will make Christian friends. They should seek out a Sunday
school class of their age group, or a singles class, and become
active. Someone should warn them not to expect the church
to be perfect, for it is largely made up of former sinners, and
many of them are also young in the faith and just leaving their
former way of life. Quite possibly they may be as much in

need of deliverance from their binding sin pattern as homosexuals.

**Twelve.
Become Active
in a Weekly
Bible Study.** In recent years home Bible studies have become quite popular. Find one, preferably one sponsored by your church, where home study assignments are administered. Ask your pastor's advice about those not definitely tied into your church. Some new converts are fortunate to have access to a weekly Bible study for former homosexuals. This is particularly beneficial during the first few weeks after conversion, but most individuals would profit by moving on to a regular group within two or three months. Or better yet, attend one Bible study for homosexuals and one for others. My reason for this suggestion is that the sooner a homosexual stops thinking of himself as "different" and accepts the fact that he is a regular person, the better off he will be. It is a happy day for a converted homosexual when he discovers a wholesome friendship love with another person of the same sex. Because there are approximately twenty heterosexuals for every homosexual Christian, the chances for close friendships are obviously much greater in a regular group.

Admittedly, many Christians who work with homosexuals advocate getting new converts active in a group made up almost exclusively of former homosexuals, and they may be right. It seems to me, however, that after a few weeks or months it is best to avoid such exclusive relationships. Paul said, "Forgetting those things that are behind . . . I press toward the mark . . ." (Philippians 3:13, 14). Exclusive fellowship with former homosexuals is apt to force the new convert to spend too much time dwelling on the past or commiserating with former homosexuals at the expense of new and unrestricted friendships.

The testimony of a man who ministers to homosexuals

tells a heartmoving story of a friendship with two heterosexual young men soon after his conversion. The day came when he felt he must take them into his confidence and tell them honestly about his past, even at the risk of losing their friendship. You can imagine his joy when they responded that they had known it all along (no one told them; they just sensed it) and loved him anyway. Until then it was hard for him to believe that straight people could really love homosexuals. Jesus Christ does make a difference!

Thirteen. Vigorously Seek Christian Companionship.

God formed man with a basic craving for fellowship with God and his fellow man (male and female). Because friendship is a risky business and everyone gets "hurt" occasionally in life, many unwisely do not develop close relationships. Former homosexuals tend to read far more into hurtful experiences than is really there. It is natural for them to be quite "testy" and defensive, assuming their background is the cause of rejection, when it may actually have nothing to do with it. (Melancholies, particularly, have a problem with suspicion anyway.) But the alternative to developing friendships is loneliness—and that's a tough pill for anyone to swallow.

In order to write this book, I had to "shelve" a book on loneliness that I had already started. My preliminary research indicates that this growing epidemic is the leading cause of suicide today. Who needs that empty feeling that follows the unrealized yearning for fellowship? Certainly not a converted homosexual seeking to follow God and come out of his former life style. We all need other people just as they need us! Former homosexuals who forsake the gay life style without finding Christian friends to lean on often return to their old life style or become sickly recluses, and some even turn suicidal.

The best place to find Christian friends is in church, Bible studies, and related Christian activity. If you are not an outgoing person and prefer solitude, push yourself; learn to be friendly. Get involved.

**Fourteen.
Find One or
More Intimate
Friends.**

All people hunger for several levels of friendship, one of which is best called "intimate other": that person or persons (usually not more than three) with whom you can share your inner self. This is not a friendship you give away easily and it takes time to develop. It is most fully realized when you sense that you are genuinely more interested in the other person and his well-being than you are your own. This unselfish love is a giving experience that enriches the giver more than the recipient.

Such a love is not necessarily sexual. Although it often appears in a husband-wife love, it can also take the form of male-male and woman-woman; however, it will not involve sex. David and Jonathan enjoyed such a relationship, for the Bible says their affection for each other surpassed that of the love of women. David married, fathered children, and knew heterosexual love, but his love for Jonathan was unique between men. Such a love usually causes a person to exclaim, "I would lay down my life for such a friend." Jonathan and David's love was not a homosexual relationship, but an enriching, sacrificing experience that is usually reserved for a small number of intimate friends. Time and common interests determine how many can be included in that intimate circle. But everyone needs one or more "best friends."

A former homosexual would be wise to seek that kind of friendship only among Christian straights who possess the same spiritual motivation and interest in the things of the Lord that he has. Remember, such a relationship does not occur instantly. He will probably need to acquire many friends, some closer than others, before a friend or two "that sticketh closer than a brother" (Proverbs 18:24) appear. Don't force it. If you remain genuinely friendly and interested in others, committing the matter to God, someone who needs your companionship will be drawn to you. Such friends will cost you something, but in the long run they are well worth the price.

Fifteen. Give Check-Up Privileges to One or More Friends.

Until you become strong in your new-found faith, it would be wise to find at least one mature friend who knows about your past and to whom you give the right to check up on you at any time. That is, you allow him to ask you privately whenever he wishes if you have remained straight, if you are avoiding the old haunts, and how your relationship with God is progressing. At first this can be your pastor, counselor, or the person who led you to Christ. It should definitely be a mature Christian whom you respect and who will protect your confidence, acting in love.

One man I counseled years ago sincerely wanted to rid himself of this awful sin. He promised me he would never again go to the city park, which he had previously frequented to meet other men. As a further means of motivation he agreed that in his best interest I could privately, but at any time, ask, "Have you been near the park lately?" Later he confided, "It was a real help when I was tempted to know that every now and then you would look me in the eye and ask that question." It is possible to break the habit without such a friend, but it makes it much easier if you have one.

Sixteen. Believe God for an Unlimited Future.

In all honesty, there is no guarantee you will ever become heterosexual. There is, however, every expectation that as a new creature in Christ Jesus you will break the bondage of homosexuality, if you follow the preceding suggestions, particularly steps 5, 6, and 7. But it is important that you do not rule out the possibility of a deep love relationship with a member of the opposite sex. If you say, "I could never respond normally to a woman," you won't! Your body will obey your mind. On the other hand, don't force it. If God wants to send you such a companion, and that is definitely a possibility, don't negate his plan by deciding in advance it is impossible. "Commit your way unto the Lord, trust also in him, and he will bring it to pass" (Psalm 37:5).

On the other hand, you may be called on to live an asexual life. Because of the complexities of our culture, the fact that women outnumber men, and fewer men are marrying than in previous decades, there are millions of singles today. The Apostle Paul lived such a life and continually testified to the availability of God's grace.

Seventeen. Present Your Body Formally to God.

As a Christian, you need to understand that Jesus Christ purchased your body by taking your sin upon himself and dying for it on the cross. Once more consider these words carefully:

"What! know ye not that your body is the temple of the Holy Spirit which is in you, which ye have of God, and ye are not your own? For ye are bought with a price: therefore glorify God in your body, and in your spirit, which are God's" (1 Corinthians 6:19, 20). Yes, God wants your body. Satan does too, and he will tempt you every way he can, particularly since he once controlled you completely. But you must realize that you have been purchased with the blood of Christ and are therefore his servant to obey, not Satan's. The choice is always yours. As a Christian, formally give your body, talents, mind, and future to God.

> I beseech you therefore, brethren, by the mercies of God, that ye present your bodies

a living sacrifice, holy, acceptable unto God, which is your reasonable service (Romans 12:1). Likewise reckon ye also yourselves to be dead indeed unto sin, but alive unto God through Jesus Christ our Lord. Let not sin therefore reign in your mortal body, that ye should obey it in the lusts thereof. Neither yield ye your members as instruments of unrighteousness unto sin: but yield yourselves unto God, as those that are alive from the dead, and your members as instruments of righteousness unto God. For sin shall not have dominion over you: for ye are not under the law, but under grace. What then? shall we sin, because we are not under the law, but under grace? God forbid. Know ye not, that to whom ye yield yourselves servants to obey, his servants ye are to whom ye obey; whether of sin unto death, or of obedience unto righteousness? But God be thanked, that ye were the servants of sin, but ye have obeyed from the heart that form of doctrine which was delivered you. Being then made free from sin, ye became the servants of righteousness (Romans 6:11-18).

The best way to do this effectively is to visualize yourself (in prayer) lying on an altar, just like the one Abraham prepared for his son Isaac. See yourself in your mind's eye on that altar, and tell your Heavenly Father in Jesus' name that you are 100 percent his, now and for eternity. Then as his servant, explicitly obey every direction. Whenever you forget to obey him, or if you willfully break that commitment, resubmit yourself to doing his will.

Eighteen. Become a People-Helper.

Because Christianity is a living faith, Spirit-controlled Christians share their faith (Acts 1:8). God has used others in your life to help you out of this sinful life style. As soon as you are able, learn to share your faith. Most good Bible-teaching churches provide teaching programs that will enable you to witness to your faith in Christ. I do not recommend that you publicly testify to having been homosexual except at special conferences for homosexuals or in selected situations. Because many well-meaning Christians still do not know how to handle such news, it would be more beneficial to refer to your past life of sin generally, just as others refer to theirs. We don't expect converted prostitutes to detail their past, and neither should you. All sin leads to a miserable life. Christ has realistically saved you from that life, so you have much to praise him for. It is not wise to spend much time telling about your past anyway. What Jesus Christ means to you now is of much greater interest to others and can be a source of blessing.

Don't be surprised if God gives you a ministry with homosexuals when you are spiritually strong enough to handle it. 2 Corinthians 1:4 instructs us that we are able to comfort others in trouble with "the same comfort with which we ourselves are comforted of God." As a pastor I have found that the greatest therapy in the world is helping others. It not only benefits those we help but richly rewards the helper. It gets his eyes off himself and onto other needy souls around him, which is healthy. Nothing is more unhealthy than a self-centered, self-obsessed thought pattern.

What about Demons?

Some who work with homosexuals are convinced they are demon possessed and must have demons removed to assure a permanent cure. Exciting stories are told of demons cast out and instant cures effected. I must confess that my experience with demons is very limited and, quite frankly, I want to keep it that way. I have a great respect for the power of the adversary, too much to engage him unnecessarily in combat.

No doubt some homosexuals are indeed demon possessed. I have seen demonstrations of militant homosexuals who appeared abnormally ''possessed.'' Sexual excesses claimed by some homosexuals seem so abnormal that they may well be motivated by demons. Certainly any person who willfully defies God and his laws for a protracted period of time is vulnerable to demon possession. But personally, I have found that blaming a person's sin (no matter what its expression) on Satan may become a copout that puts the responsibility for one's behavior on someone else and that hinders the healing process. Even after a demon is cast out, if indeed that is necessary, the individual still has to overcome the homosexuality that caused him to become so rebellious toward God that he made himself vulnerable to the demons in the first place.

I am confident of two things in this regard. First, if demon possession is involved, those leading the individual to Christ will be aware of it. Demon possession cannot permanently be hidden. Sooner or later Satan will betray his presence to the spiritually discerning. Second, God will always guide Satan's victims to a mature Christian who can assist in such matters if they are sincerely seeking God's help (John 7:17).

Summary.

Forsaking the life style of homosexuality is not easy. It will probably be the most difficult struggle a Christian homosexual has ever faced. But with God's help he can win the battle. Although their deliverance has not been advertised (or propagandized), hundreds have made such a recovery through faith in Jesus Christ. Following the above steps to victory has opened the door to a whole new productive and happy life style for many. Hopefully it will do the same for you or those you wish to help.

"I can do all things through Christ, who strengthens me"
(Philippians 4:13). Notice the first three words of that verse,
"I can do." God will not do for you what you can do for
yourself. It is unrealistic for a homosexual to expect that
receiving Jesus Christ is going to relieve him of all temptation.
I heard of one homosexual who claimed that "since Jesus
Christ didn't remove my homosexual temptation after I
became a Christian, I concluded it was a gift from God and
that he wanted me to continue that life style." That isn't even
a lie of the devil. It is self-deception, which is worse. God
wants you to quit homosexuality just as much as he wants
adulterers to stop their adultery after they become Christians.

You will be tempted to sin; that is almost certain. But God
expects you to resist the temptation. That is why we have such
scriptural challenges as "Put off the old man" and "Let not
sin have dominion over you." All sin (including
homosexuality) presents us with an option. With God's help
you can choose to obey him or reject his power for victory and
do as you please. It is not wrong to have a homosexual urge
or temptation. Many people do. A homosexual is one who
allows his urges to be fanned into passions by fantasizing or
thinking about them until he commits a homosexual act.

On a radio program a psychiatrist once cautioned, "There
is no such thing as an uncontrollable impulse. The same
muscles which pick up the gun can stop you from pulling the
trigger." God has guaranteed *never* to permit you to be
tempted above your ability to control the temptation. "There
hath no temptation taken you but such as is common to man:
but God is faithful, who will not suffer you to be tempted
above that ye are able; but will with the temptation also make
a way to escape, that ye may be able to bear it" (1 Corinthians
10:13).

CHAPTER EIGHT

The Church and the Homosexual

The church of Jesus Christ affects the moral tone of any community when she is willing to face her responsibility to minister to the whole man. However, we must recognize three kinds of churches. First, the liberal church which has no convictions because she does not believe in the authority and reliability of Scripture. Such a church (or religious club, depending on your point of view) adapts its morals to the changing standards of society. These churches usually endorse homosexuality as an optional life style. Second, some Bible-believing churches cry out for morality as a key to happiness and will condemn homosexuality as a sin. Third, other Bible-believing churches avoid contending for the Faith and ignore immorality, hoping somehow that it will all go away.

Liberal Endorsements of Homosexuality

As incredible as it may seem, many liberal churches ignore the condemnations of God on homosexuality and advocate that homosexual Christians be recognized and approved for church

143

membership. One of the nation's leading old-line
denominations (although liberalism in recent years is
contributing to its demise) incurred the wrath of some of its
laymen when it published a Sunday school quarterly favorable
to homosexuality. Ignoring the Scriptures, the publication
blandly announced, "Homosexuality is neither sin nor
sickness." It went on to develop the idea that "homosexuality
and lesbianism are normal in the sense that lefthandedness
is normal." (Anyone familiar with homosexuality literature
will recognize that this was borrowed from humanistically
oriented theoreticians who have no time for God or the Bible.
The Sunday school quarterly writer may have been unaware
of it, but he permitted himself to serve as the vehicle for
writing the devil's humanistic concepts into religious
literature.) As one of the laymen of that denomination noted,
"It is ironic that at the same time older youth and adults
were studying that in their Sunday school lesson, they read in
the newspapers the unfolding story of shocking tortures and
mass murders of young boys—the victims of violence
associated with homosexual lust." One layman was upset
because the newspaper accounts reminded him of the Bible's
description of the quality of social life found in Sodom, and
Paul's description in the first chapter of Romans of the
corruption and violence in the pagan world of his day.
According to him, "the Sunday school material condones
what the Bible calls 'abomination.' "

The above-mentioned denomination, with less than two
million adherents, is not alone. The second largest
denomination in the United States entered into a controversy,
as did two other old-line liberal groups, over the ordination
of homosexual ministers. One of their official youth
magazines challenged the church to declare that "sexual
orientation shall not be a bar to the ordained ministry."

Liberal churches and councils of churches in the last few
years have published books and pamphlets under the guise of

"understanding the homosexual." In each of these products
the pattern is the same: 1) they disregard the clear biblical
condemnations on the subject; 2) they erroneously assume that
"homosexuals are born that way" or "they can't help it" or
"they can't change"; and 3) in the name of Christian
compassion they suggest that the church "stop persecuting
homosexuals and recognize them as brothers and sisters in
Christ." Such false teachings by religious leaders remind me
of the indictment of our Lord on the Pharisees, whom he
denounced as "whited sepulchers full of dead men's bones"
and "blind leaders of the blind." Any church that publicly
condones this kind of deviant perversion removes its last
vestige of Christian reliability and is deserving of neither
support nor affiliation.

The last thing an unrepentant homosexual needs is to have
his church endorse his deviant behavior. Admittedly he does
not deserve caustic condemnation, for he is usually filled with
self-recrimination and guilt already, but he certainly doesn't
need to have his God-given guilt consciousness anesthetized
by religious falsehoods. As Jesus Christ said, it is truth that
makes you free—not deception.

Liberal churchmen not only betray their ignorance of and
unbelief in the Word of God by their excessively lenient
position on homosexuality, but they also reveal that they do
not understand its true source. The present wave of
homosexual behavior that will grow in our culture (unless
checked) is not a spontaneous phenomenon. It is the end result
of the idolatrous religion of man's humanistic wisdom. Since
current Western thought is based on the wisdom of atheistic
humanism (which the Bible labels "foolishness"), it of
necessity has come to deify man, who serves as the center
of the intellectual's world. Therefore, man owes no allegiance
to anyone above him and ought to be permitted to lay aside
all restraints on his behavior. Recall his favorite maxims—
"Do your own thing," "Do what you feel like doing," or

"Anything you want to do that doesn't hurt someone else is all right." It is bad enough when this atheistic amorality is taught at taxpayers' expense to our high school and college young people by school teachers, but it is tragic when inculcated at the expense of tithes and offerings by church leaders!

Christ and Homosexuality

The church of Jesus Christ receives its marching orders from him. Even most liberals admit that. Whether they mean it or not is questionable since they often ignore his teachings, particularly with regard to homosexuality. Anyone who feels our Lord kept silent on the subject of homosexuality is misinformed.

Those who try to defend homosexuality usually maintain that condemnation of homosexuality is an Old Testament teaching. Because Christ came to free us from the Law, and since he did not discuss same-sex union, we are no longer under the Old Testament condemnatory policy, they insist. What they forget is that the Old Testament reveals God's attitude toward sin, so that the fact that we do not stone people for homosexual acts today does not change the fact that in God's righteous eyes it is still an "abomination "

Male-Female Sex in Marriage Is the Only Sex Christ Approved. Christ came not to destroy the Law but, as he said, "to fulfill it." The only time he adjusted Old Testament Law was when he raised the standard, as he did in the Sermon on the Mount, when he elevated the standard from lust to adultery or hatred to murder. By no stretch of the imagination would he have lowered the Old Testament teachings on homosexuality. Because it was not a common problem in that day in Israel (stoning then kept it to a minimum), he did not address it directly. However, three of his teachings imply his attitude of condemnation.

First, male-female sex in marriage is the normal biblical pattern, "But from the beginning of the creation God made them male and female" (Mark 10:6).

The sexual union of man and woman in marriage is always approved in Scripture. The sexual union of male with male or female with female is never approved, but is always condemned when mentioned (see Romans 1:27). Therefore, his exclusion of homosexuality signifies that he approved its prohibition in Scripture.

Second, "fornication" was condemned by Christ, and homosexuality is a form of fornication. "And I say unto you, Whosoever shall put away his wife, except it be for fornication, and shall marry another, committeth adultery; and whoso marrieth her which is put away doth commit adultery" (Matthew 19:9).

The Greek word for fornication is *porneia*, which means giving one's self to unlawful sex with another. Jude 7 uses that same word to describe the sins of Sodom and Gomorrah "Fornication" does not exclusively mean homosexual sin, for it usually refers to male-female sex out of marriage. But the Jude 7 passage clearly refers to homosexuality, and this is condemned by Christ in the above text.

Third, Christ's warning about Sodom and Gomorrah indicates his attitude. "Likewise also as it was in the days of Lot; they did eat, they drank, they bought, they sold, they planted, they builded; but the same day that Lot went out of Sodom it rained fire and brimstone from heaven, and destroyed them all" (Luke 17:28, 29).

Our Lord here acknowledges the destruction of Sodom and Gomorrah for their sins. Since he had access only to the Hebrew account in Genesis, he obviously knew, as the Jews have always recognized, that the specific sin of those cities had been homosexuality. His warning here, then, not only involves his approval of their condemnation to destruction for homosexuality, but predicts that similar conditions will exist in the last days just before his return.

The Lord Jesus didn't say much about homosexuality, but he certainly said enough. For instance, only twice did he command, "You must be born again," yet all Bible-believing Christians accept that. Why, then, should any question his three teachings above which outlaw homosexuality as an alternative life style for Christians?

Compassion or Condemnation

The Bible is so clear in its condemnation of homosexuality (bear in mind, it also condemns adultery, lying, stealing, etc.), as we saw in a previous chapter, that those churches and Christians who take God's Word literally have no difficulty deciding whether or not homosexuality is right or wrong. But just denouncing homosexuality as sin is certainly not the church's only responsibility in the face of this growing epidemic. Homosexuals are people and people are sinners. Therefore, from eight to ten million homosexual sinners in our country need the compassion of Christ reflected through the church and its people by their communication of the gospel and its remedy for their chosen life style.

The prejudice and hatred toward homosexuals on the part of Christians who have never harbored a homosexual impulse is appalling, existing even among some who teach that Spirit-controlled Christians must show love and compassion toward their fellow man. Recently a pastor's wife told me she had been summoned for jury duty on a case involving a homosexual. While waiting to be interviewed, she heard a Bible-believing minister questioned by the defense attorney to determine his eligibility to serve as a juror. The attorney asked, "Do you have any convictions about homosexuality?" "Yes, sir, I do!" was the minister's reply. "I believe it is ungodly and sinful, and I can't stomach it. I have absolutely no respect for any homosexual!" The attorney then asked, "Do you mean as a person or as a man?" To which the minister replied, "I mean as a person. God made them male and female, and that's it!"

Such an attitude certainly does not reflect the spirit of our Lord, who welcomed and ministered to tax collectors, prostitutes, adulterers, and other sinners. Admittedly, he told them to "Go and sin no more," but he loved them as persons. Can Christians today do less?

It is important in this connection to distinguish between homosexuality and homosexuals. All true Christians should oppose homosexuality, for it is wrong and exceedingly dangerous to society. But it is inaccurate to lump all homosexuals into one category. They are different as all people are different. As you consider the following varieties of homosexuals, you will find that each one is unique and should be treated differently.

1. The unhappy Gay.

2. The Christian whose conscience constantly plagues him.

3. The Christian who fights homosexual temptations every day of his life.

4. The deceived homosexual. Millions fall into this category, for they have been duped by society, education, and religion into thinking that homosexuality is acceptable, though they still feel guilt, loneliness, depression, etc.

5. The former homosexual Christian who lets his guard down and falls into sin.

6. The defiant deviant.

7. The militant homosexual.

The Christian who cannot muster at least a little compassion

for homosexual sinners either has a spiritual problem himself
or has never personally met a troubled homosexual. I must
confess, until I was brought face-to-face with a person who
acknowledged this deviant life style, it was hard for me to
reach out an arm of compassion. When your closest contact
with a homosexual person involves observing a "queen"
dressed in full "drag" on a public street, it is easy to be
intolerant. But when that same queen comes to you and pours
out his heart, describing the miserable existence he calls
"life," you would have to possess a heart of stone not to be
moved by his obvious need.

The church of Jesus Christ should always show
compassion, even when it is obliged to oppose sin and sinners.
But we must get over the idea that extending compassion
to a homosexual is an indication of compromise.
Homosexuality is a blight on humanity, but homosexuals
are sinners who desperately need Jesus Christ, and we will
never reach them with his love until we first extend them
our own.

Most homosexuals tell me they are generally rejected by
Christians, even when they attend church. Of course,
homosexuals are often supersensitive and suspicious, so they
may well read occasional church unfriendliness as rejection
of their life style. But anyone who would work with
homosexuals (and certainly that includes the church, which
proceeds under Christ's mandate to preach the gospel to
"the whole world") had better face the fact that they have an
enormous need to be loved. Their lifetime patterns of rejection
will naturally make them suspicious, so we must compensate
for that by seeking the power of God's Spirit to extend
"compassion" (biblical love) to them. I have found that
dealing with them personally greatly aids my understanding
of the problem. The more aloof you remain from a
homosexual person, the easier it is to hate both him and his
sin. The closer you get, the easier it is to distinguish
between the sinner and his sin.

If a holy and righteous God could appear personally to the chief of sinners, who described himself as a "blasphemer, persecutor, and injurious," then certainly God can love homosexuals. With all due respect to Saul of Tarsus, I can hardly believe that a man or woman who practices a form of sexual inversion is worse than the man who stoned to death the leading first-century preacher, who persecuted and possibly killed many other Christians. The church should be as ready to extend the love, mercy, and grace of God to a homosexual as it is to condemn his sinful sex life. With a homosexual community that now numbers eight to ten million, and with a climate that promises to double those numbers in the next decade, we in the church had better recognize this potent force of troubled souls and create a church atmosphere that assures them of our love. If we fail them, they are hopeless in this life and the life to come.

Militant Christian Compassion

Christians are "the salt of the earth," but when salt has lost its "savor" (saltiness), it is worthless and fit only to be thrown out. During the past fifty years or so the church of Jesus Christ has been lulled to sleep with the strange idea that the moral atmosphere of our society is not its responsibility. Consequently, the amoral worshipers of atheistic humanism have had more influence on the moral climate of society than Christians. We have focused almost exclusively on "saving the world by preaching the gospel" while the humanists have gone about lowering standards. We said little as they lowered the waiting period for divorce—now we have one divorce for every two marriages. We said little when they abolished capital punishment—now we have become the crime capital of the world. A few Christian "extremists" objected when humanism led the attack on clean literature, and now we are flooded with pornography. Objections to drugs, permissive sex, and a host of other vices were scarcely heard even when laws against homosexual activity were struck down and replaced with "consorting laws" so that homosexuals could freely practice their favorite form of perversion "in private."

Finally some Christians were stirred by the militant Christian compassion of Anita Bryant and Dr. Jerry Falwell in Dade County, Florida, and the homosexual steamroller was temporarily stalled. Maybe, just maybe, the possibility of having homosexual role models as school teachers is the alarm buzzer that has awakened sleeping Christians. Perhaps paying a school teacher's salary to exalt homosexuality as a wholesome alternative to marriage and the family will motivate Christians to use their God-given American freedoms to pass legislation that will protect innocent school children from being victimized by this false notion that the un-gay life is gay. It should be vigorously opposed by every Christian (who claims the name of Jesus Christ) in the name of Christian compassion.

Christian compassion? you may ask. Yes, Christian compassion. It is not compassion that causes a Christian to stand idly by while a few militant homosexuals create a climate that will sweep additional millions of victims into this macabre way of life. It is laziness, or in some cases even worse—cowardice. If our Lord were living in America today, I have no doubt he would speak out vigorously and frequently against this blight on humanity. And he certainly wouldn't have waited until a godly woman led the way.

Anita Bryant Green deserves the admiration and thanks of every Christian American for her courageous fight against homosexuality in her community. In spite of the innuendoes and misrepresentations of her motives and methods by the homosexual-loving press and media in our country, she is a Christian to be respected and imitated. As the founder of the largest Christian high school in California, I do not want to be forced by law to hire a homosexual school teacher on any level. Nor do I as a taxpayer want to subsidize their further deterioration of the public school. And it is Christian compassion for the future innocent victims of this sin that makes me say so. Like Anita, I love homosexuals, but I hate their sinful life style that contagiously reaches into the minds of otherwise normal young people. The last thing a young person with a predisposition toward homosexuality needs is a false climate of respectability created for homosexuality, inducing him to experiment with it rather than save himself for marriage, as he is clearly instructed to do in the Bible.

What You Can Do

You may well ask, "What can I as a Christian do about this evil?" As a pastor for twenty-eight years and a Christian educator for fifteen, I would like to urge you to get up out of your church pews (after the services are over!) and *do* something about the problem. Too long have we sat idly by, doing nothing. It is time to get involved with our society and stop this madness. The following suggestions are offered with the hope that many will act on them.

1. Write short incisive letters to every local, state, and national official who votes on these matters.

2. Encourage other Christians to do the same.

3. If legal in your state, help organize an initiative petition to your state constitution, prohibiting homosexuals from becoming school teachers.

4. Work for the election of Christians and other politicians who openly endorse Christian standards of morality.

5. Add to your prayer list the request that Christian men and women offer themselves to God and their country to run for every elective office in the land, from local school board and city council positions to U.S. Representatives and

Senators. Too long have we slept quietly while a large number
of humanistically brainwashed people have been swept into
office with few moral convictions. The mess we are in today
has been brought on through legislation by amoral legislators,
and it will be cleaned up only when we elect representatives
who share our Christian standards of morality.

6. Encourage your minister to read this book and
prayerfully urge him (if he is not already doing so) to lead your
congregation in opposing this and other immoral evils in your
community. If the church doesn't oppose the increase in evil,
who will?

7. Watch your local schools to see that no teacher is
permitted to exalt homosexual life styles in the classroom.
And if any teacher's homosexuality is revealed, or if he boldly
comes out of the closet to parade his deviant sex life, gather
a group of Christians together and present the matter to the
principal. If he refuses to take action, then refer the matter
to the school board, and, if need be, to the State
Superintendent of Education. Remember, if we lose the battle
with homosexuals in the school room, we have lost the battle!

8. Do what you can through your local church to win lost
homosexuals to Jesus Christ. Befriend them and help them
out of their unhappy life style.

Don't Persecute Homosexuals

Christians should never persecute other human beings. For
that reason our love for individuals should always be manifest
in our actions, even our militant Christian compassion. We do
not wish to persecute homosexuals. We are, however,
opposed to the propagation of their life style by perverting
our children, which is the only way their sterile system can
continue. Prohibiting their opportunity to teach school is not
persecuting them; it is protecting our children, who constitute

our first priority. We don't oppose homosexuals' seeking
employment in other fields in life, with over 100 vocations
to choose from. But if they decide to adopt a homosexual life
style, then they have no business in the classroom, particularly
at taxpayers' expense. If they wish to teach school, they have
three alternatives:

1. Stop being homosexual—that is their choice.

2. Organize a school for homosexuals taught by
homosexuals and paid for by homosexuals and their
supporters.

3. Pass legislation which will enable them to maintain
their perverted life style while teaching children produced
by heterosexuals.

It is this latter procedure which they have chosen to follow
and which we should oppose with compassion and diligence.
Our parents passed on to us a heterosexual culture; in a few
generations there well may be no grandchildren.

Some Christians may ask, "Pastor LaHaye, won't this
kind of militance destroy the influence of our church and limit
our soulwinning effectiveness?" To save you the time it
would take to write me a letter, I will give my answer here.
Such moral action will probably stir up a few noisy dissenters,
but we have found in our church that it attracts far more who
agree with Christian morals but are not Christians yet. This
country, like any other, is made up largely of "sheep without
a shepherd." And consequently they have been following the
amoral humanists in sheep's clothing so long that even many
of them are becoming alarmed. The Dade County vote of 69
percent was representative of non-church people, Christians,
Jews, blacks, and many others who oppose homosexuals'
being paid to teach school where they can corrupt innocent
children. Such people will have greater respect for Christ and
his church if we will come out of our churches after services
and lead them back into a moral America. Many will also
receive our Lord personally. But almost all would rather live
in a safe and sexually normal community.

What to Do When Your Child Announces "I'm Gay!"

The priority for most parents is that their children grow up to be healthy, happy, normal members of society who marry and eventually produce another generation. In our society this is particularly true of the country's largest minority group, ''born-again Christians.'' Our major objective is to raise children to glorify God. Many such parents would prefer the death of their child to his adopting the unhappy wretchedness of homosexuality.

We live today in a climate conducive to homosexuality. It is flaunted in the home on TV, homosexual pornography is readily available to anyone with the money to buy it; and X-rated movies exalt lesbian heroines and homosexual male idols. Many sex education teachers are neutral on the morality of homosexuality, and some have been accused of openly endorsing it as a legitimate life style. Now that homosexuality has gone militant and politicians are being intimidated into striking down traditional laws against it, Christian families cannot expect to go unscathed. No one knows, of course, how many of the eight to ten million homosexuals in America came from Christian homes, but you can be sure of one thing—in every case it has produced heartrending tragedy.

In some cases the "announcement" or the discovery does
not come as a complete shock because obviously
"effeminate" mannerisms, disinterest in girls, and spiritual
lethargy served as a warning to discerning parents. As we have
seen, however, all effeminate-acting males are not
homosexuals, and all homosexuals are not effeminate.
Consequently, many Christian parents are caught totally
unprepared and often react emotionally.

Christian Life magazine carried a series of articles on
homosexuality earlier this year. I was deeply moved by one
story written by a mother who signed her report
"Anonymous." She told the story of her handsome nineteen-
year-old son who had been "Mr. Everything" through school.
In addition, he was a popular, dedicated Christian who
had won several young people to Christ. One day she
accidentally discovered his secret pile of homosexual
magazines stuffed under the bed. Crushed and distraught,
she and her husband confronted him with the evidence. Their
son defiantly screamed, "I hate you!" and ran out of their
lives for eleven months.

A few weeks later I wrote to several of the effective
Christian ministries to homosexuals around the country,
telling them I was doing research for this book and requesting
any help they could supply. My letter was passed on to this
mother, who wrote me a warm and informative five-page
letter. You can imagine my astonishment when I discovered
that she was a beautiful Christian college classmate of many
years ago whom I could never quite get up enough nerve
to ask for a date. Although I had lost all contact with her, I
remembered her as a talented, bubbly, personable, outgoing
Sanguine with a deep commitment to Christ and beloved by
everyone.

That was the first time it occurred to me that Christian
parents could be devastated by this problem. This is how she
described it:

It all seemed unreal. In recent years fads among young people have run the gamut. First came booze. In the 1960s it was drugs. Today knowledgeable youth workers say the "in thing" is bisexuality, even hard-core homosexuality! But could homosexuality actually touch the child of Christians? I hadn't even known what a homosexual was until I was in my 20s. And only two months before our confrontation with our son, when I'd heard that a local youth advisor at a camp for runaway boys was a homosexual, I had announced rather loudly to the family, "I'd rather die than have that happen!"

Now our son was involved with another boy his age!

Suddenly, all we knew was what we felt: complete, uncomprehending shock, mingled with confused disbelief. We didn't realize then that homosexuality wasn't something you could turn off like a light switch. And although we tried to convey our love for our son, our overreaction must have come across as a condemnation.

"You're not my mother! I never want to see you again," he said.

We've learned firsthand that Christians are not immune to homosexuality. We've also learned that we are not the sole survivors but part of a growing minority of shattered parents in the process of being healed by God. And God is able to work beauty out of the ugliness of sin—even out of homosexuality. But it takes time and praise and the power of prayer to surrender to God what somehow seems too painful to bear.

Terminally ill patients often struggle with denial, anger, and depression before they can accept their own approaching death. But for the Christian, death is ultimately a victory where we finally face our Lord. The reactions of a parent whose child has labeled himself a homosexual often parallel these initial traumatic reactions, but the emotional loss of a child to homosexuality is more far-reaching. It affects one with physical symptoms of anxiety, chest pains, nausea. It becomes a living grief with an uncertain end, a daily shouldering of self-blame that only God can alleviate, and the nightly drumbeat of "why our child?"

Those first few months after we learned about our son, I lost thirty pounds. I could hardly get up in the morning and went into a severe depression. Friends would say, "What's wrong? You're just not the same bubbly person!" But how can you be the same? I wrote reams of letters asking everyone from Billy Graham to Oral Roberts why a Christian boy could get involved, and got no positive answers. It was either too hot to handle—or no one quite knew what to say.

That's when I created my "joy box"— a shoe box stuffed with any inspirational Scripture, poems, stories and letters I could find. Within easy reach on my kitchen counter, I grab into that box for a dose of praise and hope whenever the negatives seem to outweigh the positives.

At first, there didn't seem to be anyone else in the whole world who was going through what we were suffering, or who had experienced the same tremendous emotional tug-of-war with depression and guilt! If they had, they weren't willing to discuss it. If they hadn't, they couldn't possibly understand it or handle it.

Where are all the other suffering mothers, Lord? There must be one! Just one to help me see it's possible for this wound to heal!

My friend of former years was not the only one to send a letter as a homosexual's parent. As I corresponded with a young man who had written me earlier, describing how my book *The Act of Marriage* had helped in his recent marriage

after he extricated himself from homosexuality, his mother
wrote to urge that I include this chapter in the book. No man
or woman is an island. All our lives affect other people—and
that is especially true of the parents of homosexuals.

God in his marvelous grace has used this problem in my
friend's life, and now she has an effective ministry to un-gay
mothers called "Spatula Club" in Anaheim, California. She
is doubly blessed. Her son finally returned home and has come
out of homosexuality. Because she has been there, she can
be a rich blessing to brokenhearted mothers. "Blessed be
God, even the Father of our Lord Jesus Christ, the Father of
mercies, and the God of all comfort; who comforteth us in all
our tribulation, that we may be able to comfort them which
are in any trouble, by the comfort wherewith we ourselves
are comforted of God" (2 Corinthians 1:3, 4).

As with homosexuality itself, there is no easy way to cope
with the grief. By its very nature it is painful to everyone
involved. The following suggestions from my friend and from
others who have written, and basic biblical principles will
help those who face this heartache.

Coping with
Your Child

Your child is more important than you and your feelings. His
or her life hangs in the balance, and there are some positive
steps you can take.

One.
Don't Blow Up.

When we deal with those we love,
nothing is more divisive than words.
That is particularly true of
disapproving words, especially to homosexuals. As we have
seen, they have already faced all the rejection, shame,
remorse, and guilt one person needs in a lifetime. In fact,
most homosexuals have confronted more of that by the age of

nineteen than heterosexuals experience in a lifetime. Once
said, words can never be recalled. And since homosexuals are
so filled with hate and bitterness anyway, your heated words
only complicate an already difficult scene. The Bible warns,
"Be slow to anger" and "A *soft* answer turneth away wrath."

**Two.
Love Him
or Her.**
Whether you know it or not, in the
mind of your child you are
consciously or subconsciously on
trial at that traumatic moment of
announcement. His obsession to be loved makes the
unreasoning demand, "If you really love me, you will love me
anyway." And basically he is right. It really boils down to
what you are most interested in—your reputation, your
disappointment, or his problem.

The most beautiful story I have ever heard in such a
situation involved a hard-driving Choleric father whose
Spirit-filled life caused him to react in tears instead of anger.
Putting his arms around his boy, he prayed, "O God, save my
son," and sobbed as if his heart would break. The young man
couldn't trample his father's love for long; within a month he
repented of his sin and broke with his former life style. Later
he said, "I had never seen my father cry before. For the first
time I realized he really did love me." To this day I am the
only outsider who knows that family's secret. Love triumphed
again. At the risk of sounding negative, it has been my
experience that most parents don't react like that. Remember,
"Love is the royal law in Scripture."

**Three.
Accept Him
While Rejecting
His Life Style.**
As we have explained, the
homosexual already has a difficult
time accepting himself. If you reject
him, it will only heighten his
self-rejection. He needs to know that

sink or swim, good or bad, he is your child, and *nothing* he does will ever take him out of your heart, life, or family. Once he has made his announcement, expect him to be unpredictable, even leaving rather than being able to face you again. You don't have to do one thing wrong to cause him to leave home. The guilt or sin is sufficient. What he needs to know is that "the door is always open," that he "always has a home here." That does not mean you condone his life style. He knows you disapprove, but he needs to be certain that your approval of him is greater than your censure of his sin.

Four. Protect His Confidence.

Your heart will be so heavy that you will naturally want to share your pain with friends and neighbors. Don't do it! Commit it to God, tell him, but don't betray your child's confidence. Look forward to the day he will return and try to pick up the pieces of his life. Don't make it harder for him to return by letting his secret out. Allow your child to determine how far out of the closet he wants to come.

Five. Don't Throw Him out of the House.

Hurt, angry parents are apt to order their homosexual child out of the home. This is a dreadful tactic. Such a response not only rejects him but throws him to the homosexual wolves, who are anxious to prey upon his young body. The most precious possession in your house is that child—treat him as such. If ever he needed you, it is now. Personally, I do not recommend that he be permitted to bring his homosexual friends or "lover" to your home, but certainly he himself should be welcome. Your constant prayer for his deliverance is far more likely to be answered in your home than in a homosexual environment.

**Six.
Don't Take
Him to a
Psychiatrist.**
Seek counsel with a Christian counselor who practices Christian counseling principles, never a humanistically-trained non-Christian psychiatrist or psychologist. Their ways are *not* God's ways, they are notoriously unsuccessful in the treatments they prescribe, and, personally, I have found some who give very harmful, unchristian advice. Your child needs to be screened from the "professional" who suggests it is "normal" to be abnormal.

If your child will visit a counselor, find one who is a Christian and preferably one who has had experience with homosexuals.* If you take him to your pastor, I suggest you call and warn him in advance. Some will readily admit they do not know how to counsel homosexuals. Others may prefer to review the procedure they should follow in advance of the interview. Just as your surgeon would not operate without studying a case carefully, a pastor will profit from a telephone call in order to study the issues at hand.

Coping with Yourself

Now that we have dealt with your reaction to your child, it is time to contemplate your own feelings during this traumatic experience. The world hasn't come to an end; it only seems that way. My friend's testimony and that of many others makes it clear that you will probably receive the emotional shock of your life. But this is not the time to give in to spiritual defeat. The following four steps will help you to gain the victory.

---

*For the names of recommended Christian counselors in your area, send a stamped, self-addressed envelope to: Family Life Seminars, 2100 Greenfield Drive, El Cajon, California 92021.

**One.
Don't Take the
Guilt Trip.**
The most universal response to the "I'm Gay!" announcement is "What did I do wrong?" or "Where did we fail?" Even worse, you may be inclined to ask yourself, "What will people think?" You may have made many mistakes, of course. Who hasn't? All parents are amateurs (ask any grandparent), and thus error is inescapable. But most of us didn't know any better at the time. When people tell my wife and me that they wish they had known the principles we teach when their children were little, we always respond, "So do we." Frankly, I think my son and daughter are better parents than Bev and I were, because they know far more about parenting than we did.

Blaming yourself for past mistakes won't solve anything now. In fact, it will only complicate matters. Besides, you didn't make your child homosexual; he chose that life style and can choose to leave it. Even if you made some serious mistakes, it is wrong to dwell on them. Confess them to God (1 John 1:9), then forget them. If God can forgive you, certainly you ought to be able to forgive yourself.

**Two.
Avoid
Wallowing
in Self-Pity!**
Self-pity is probably the most harmful mental thought pattern people indulge in today. It destroys joy, quenches the Spirit of God, drains your energy, and leaves you depressed. (For a full treatment of this subject, see the author's *How to Win Over Depression*.)

**Three.
Give Thanks
by Faith.**
"In everything give thanks: for this is the will of God in Christ Jesus concerning you" (1 Thessalonians 5:18).

Admittedly, it is never easy to give thanks in the midst of a heartbreak. But God does not command us to do what he won't enable us to accomplish. By faith give thanks for what God is able to accomplish in the midst of your problem. Gradually your feelings will improve.

Four. Walk in the Spirit. "This I say then, 'Walk in the Spirit, and ye shall not fulfill the lust of the flesh'" (Galatians 5:16).

If ever you needed to walk in the Spirit on a day-by-day basis, it is now. But this is not possible unless you regularly (preferably daily) read the Word of God and pray with thanksgiving, being obedient to him.

Five. Serve the Lord Faithfully. Look for opportunities to serve the Lord. This old world is so full of troubled people that you won't have to look far. You may well find that, like my friend, God will give you a ministry to others who suffer as you do. You are certainly not alone.

Six. Take an Active Part in a Bible-Believing Church That Teaches the Spirit-Filled Life. You need Christian companionship and spiritual edification. That is one of the reasons God instituted the church. It is his spiritual service station for Christians who are running low on fuel.

CHAPTER TEN

Homosexuality Gone Militant

Last night the network news carried the announcement that Anita Bryant was dropped from doing the commentary at the Orange Bowl Parade this year. Then it had the audacity to add, "Network officials say her opposition to homosexuals had nothing to do with the decision." Anyone who gives credence to that would believe Abraham Lincoln shot John Wilkes Booth.

This announcement comes on the heels of the well-publicized fiasco in Houston, where it became apparent that the E.R.A.* movement had been taken over by militant lesbians. Good women across the country were shocked to discover that at taxpayers' expense ($5 million), the program they thought would benefit women in general will really aid

*The Equal Rights Amendment has stalled three states short of passage, and three states have rescinded their votes because it is becoming clear to America's women that should it pass, it will be the greatest disservice to womanhood in American history. Most women who support it have no idea how harmful it is to straight women and how helpful to lesbians and homosexuals. For example, if it passes, it will be impossible for school boards to fire a school teacher (male or female), as the Supreme Court has just upheld an Oregon board for doing, because the teacher in question was a homosexual. The irony of the E.R.A. is that those who support it think it will provide American women with equal job opportunities (as former First Lady Ford announced in Houston). The truth is, the amendment does not provide American women one thing more than they have received in the 1972 Job Opportunity Law already on the books.

167

homosexuals in particular. Even the most liberal straights who
actively support the E.R.A. were shocked at the lesbian
literature and devices displayed at the convention. As one
woman put it, "Sexual kinks have come out of their secret
closets to demonstrate and display their wares at government-
sponsored conventions at taxpayers' expense."

Thinking people find it a bit frightening that in this land
that is supposed to guarantee "human rights," "free speech,"
and "freedom for all," we tend to insure freedom only for
the minority to speak out and overturn the majority traditional
standards. If you are a straight wife and mother who opposes
the overthrow of Judeo-Christian moral standards that have
always been a part of America, you are faced with a TV and
communications blackout. But if you are a known lesbian or
homosexual sympathizer, you can get free TV coverage. Lest
you consider that a faulty conclusion, ask yourself why
3,500 women, who had their expenses paid by the
government, received so much TV coverage while 3,000
women who oppose the E.R.A., meeting in Houston at the
same time at their own expense, were given very little
mention in the national news. Do you ever wonder sometimes
"whose team the TV medium is on, anyway"?

The present militant mood of homosexuality has caught
many Americans by surprise, but it shouldn't have. It has
been developing steadily for three decades. During that time
it has grown from an obscure subject, almost too embarrassing
to mention, to a movement which has many political
candidates falling all over themselves, trying to secure
its backing without alienating their other supporters. Even
"born-again" President Carter, who realized he would be
elected by a thin margin, did everything he could to cultivate
the homosexual vote. "He promised he would move
immediately to federally decriminalize sodomy and related
sexual acts. His stand was advertised to the homosexual

constituency in full-page advertisements appearing in gay
publications. One such ad showed the candidate's wife,
Rosalyn, engaged in conversation with two well-known gay
leaders, Troy Perry of the Metropolitan Community Church
and Dr. Newton Deiter. Gays worked actively in the Carter
campaign and endorsed him time and again."[29]

Former President Gerald Ford refused to cultivate the
homosexual vote and lost the election by three percentage
points (representing less than the registered homosexual
voters). This lesson did not go unnoticed by politicians. A
California state senator friend of mine said, "Politicians are
interested in two things: 1) getting elected to office and
2) staying in office." In the future we can expect militant
homosexuals to exert a far greater force in the political arena
than their eight to ten million numbers would indicate. In a
close political race they could well be the balance of power.

American history reveals that several notable homosexuals
have been active in society, the arts, and even in government
for over one hundred years. But it was President Franklin
D. Roosevelt's administration that seemed particularly lenient
toward them. One historian said, "Every president from
Franklin Roosevelt forward has had homosexuals in his
administration."[30]

Many readers remember the McCarthy era. Between 1947
and 1955 the well-publicized senator from Wisconsin was
instrumental in removing almost 1,100 individuals from
government for being homosexuals or because they were
suspected of being "sexual deviants." In all probability some
of these people were victims of false accusations and
inadequate evidence, but that many might have been guilty is
suggested by a statement from the head of the Washington,
D.C., Police Vice Squad, who "estimated there were five
thousand homosexuals in the nation's capitol at that time,
with thirty-seven hundred in government service."[31]

You may well be asking, "How did all this homosexual power come about in this country?" The answer is not only fascinating but reveals who has been behind it all the time. To understand the growth of homosexuality in our culture during the past thirty years, you should consider three major divisions: The Homophile Movement, the Gay Liberation Movement, and The New Alliance for Gay Equality.

The Homophile Movement

The word *homophile* comes from two Greek words, *homo* or "same," and *philos* meaning "love." The "same love" or homophile title is much nicer-sounding than "homosexual" and represents the older, seasoned, "calm" heads of the homosexual movement who have tried to change the attitude of the country towards homosexuality in an attempt to make themselves more acceptable to society. At first they went about their work quietly by producing literature that subtly reflected the homosexual life. Plays, movies, TV programs, magazines, books, and more recently school textbooks were designed to gradually turn the country around on this subject. No one can deny they succeeded very well. Perhaps 100 organizations in this movement during the past eight or ten years have become increasingly vocal, demanding, and militant.

The first organization, and perhaps the most influential of all, was "The Mattachine Society." I have read that the founder was a card-carrying member of the Communist Party for eighteen years and a popular teacher of Marxist principles who staunchly refused to deny such membership before the House Unamerican Activities Committee in 1955.[32] From the very beginning this society was organized secretly, similar to the Communist Party. Its magazine drew heavily on Kinsey and Communist literature, freely using such expressions as "sexual freedom," "police brutality," "a violation of our civil rights," and "minorities like homosexuals." Since then, the magazine has become a basic instruction manual for homosexuals around the country.

In 1957 the State of California granted non-profit status to "The Daughters of Bilitus." Together with another organization called "One," these three pioneers of the "Homophile" movement have steered America to the outskirts of Sodom and Gomorrah.

> They began to hold national conventions in major cities around the country, each more widely publicized and open than the one before. They campaigned in behalf of candidates sympathetic to gay causes. They lobbied against anti-gay laws at the state and local levels and for pro-homosexual legislation. They sought and received interviews on radio and television programs in such cities as New York, Los Angeles, San Francisco, and Denver. And they began to seek the aid of major Christian denominations.[33]

Unfortunately, they found the liberal wing of Christianity, which is often more interested in helping lost humanity do its own thing than in reconciling them to the God who loves them, only too willing to aid their cause.

On January 3, 1965, the San Francisco *Examiner* and the *Chronicle* both carried proof that the Homophile Movement had succeeded in influencing liberal clergymen, for they published the shocking tale of a fund-raising dance for 600 homosexuals, sponsored by more than six ministers and their wives. Little did the clerics and their spouses realize that among the hands they shook in the receiving line were fifty undercover agents of the San Francisco Police Department, who took pictures of the "dance." The police thought it was illegal for so many men to be dressed like women, and the ministers were taken to jail along with the homosexuals.

This New Year's ball that raised the money to start the
"Council on Religion and the Homosexual" served as the
historic "coming out party" for the homosexual movement.
The blatant approval and defense of this flaunting of
perversion by liberal ministers gave members of the
Homophile Movement reason to believe that the time had
come to demand acceptance for their chosen life style, even
though it was illegal at that time in forty-six of the fifty
states. During the next few years liberal denominations were
confronted with resolutions calling for leniency and
understanding of homosexuals. The old lies were resurrected
that "they can't help it," "they're born that way," "a child's
sexual direction is determined by the time he is five years
old" so that in the name of Christianity they could sanction
perversion. Even though a few denominations ordained
lesbians to the priesthood and defended the ordination of
homosexual ministers, most of the ministers and practically
all of the lay people rebelled at calling "Christian" what God
labels "abomination." Although they haven't given up on
religion and the churches, the homosexual boom has found far
more receptivity in the public and political sector than in the
church, even many liberal churches.

The Gay
Liberation
Movement

Thanks to the efforts of the Homophile Movement, the sexual
revolution started by Kinsey (which was methodically
cultivated by radical sex educators in the public schools), and
the anti-American, anti-establishment feeling fostered by
educators during the Viet Nam war, millions of young
homosexuals were ready to go militant. Many of them had

worked in the Civil Rights Movement, not because they loved the blacks, but because they shared their plight of "discrimination" and because they were angry and wanted to rebel anyway. The success of the black community after enactment of civil rights legislation in 1964 was not lost on the homosexuals. They realized that they could force acceptance on sleeping Americans if they became active. They got their chance in New York City.

June 27th, 1969, is another "red" letter day in the rise to prominence of the homosexual movement. That was the night the New York City Police raided a homosexual bar called "Stonewall Inn." Instead of slinking off into the night, homosexuals threw bottles and cans at policemen, and a riot ensued. Now each year a "Gay Pride Week" is celebrated with a giant parade in New York, San Francisco, Los Angeles, and other cities. They wear T-shirts identifying themselves as homosexual and carry signs blatantly announcing, "Gay Is Good" or "Two-four-six-eight, Gay is just as good as Straight."

Not all homosexuals are militant, even many whose sexual life is out in the open. Most of the young militants seriously concern the older homosexuals, for they fear that all this militancy will create a backlash that may cost them hard-earned victories. Today they have most of the things they want: privacy, vocational acceptance in most fields, and very little harassment by the police at their favorite bar or bath. The hot-blooded young homosexuals aren't satisfied, however, for their ultimate goal has still eluded them: equal acceptance! Until Americans say "Gay is just as good as straight," they won't give up. Four thousand gay bars, free access to baths, and their own churches are not enough. They demand equal recognition of sexual perversion. Some militants wouldn't even be satisfied with equal status if it came to them. One of them, quoted in the *New York Times*, said,

> The older groups are oriented toward
> getting accepted by the establishment, but
> what the establishment has to offer me
> isn't worth my time. We aren't oriented
> toward acceptance, but toward changing
> every institution in this country; male
> domination, capitalist exploitation, and all
> the rest of it.

In 1972 a meeting of several homosexual groups in the Gay Liberation Movement met in Chicago and mapped out the following plan of operation:

1. Repeal of all state laws prohibiting private sexual acts involving consenting persons.

2. Repeal of all laws governing the age of consent for sexual acts.

3. Creation of sex education courses taught by homosexuals and presenting homosexuality as a valid, healthy life style and a viable alternative to heterosexuality.

4. Adoption of legislation prohibiting discrimination against homosexuals in employment, housing, public accommodations, and public services.

Since that meeting, over seventeen states and many cities have created just such laws and struck down many traditional statutes based on our Judeo-Christian moral code. In addition, they have hounded many good politicians out of office, including a personal Christian friend of mine who had been a State Assemblyman from Orange County for ten years. They threatened to "get" him and made good their threat in 1976.

In November 1973, the American Psychiatric Association, meeting in Washington, D. C., removed homosexuality from the category of mental illness. Instead they created a new category, "Sexual Orientation Disturbance," referring to "individuals whose sexual interests are directed primarily toward people of the same sex," and they advocated that homosexuality be considered merely one form of sexual behavior.

In fairness to the field of psychiatry, it should be noted that the resolution passed by a narrow margin and has been vigorously opposed by many of the country's leading psychiatrists. Several from the Menninger Foundation stump the country, warning that some sexually sick people running around now are labeled "normal." Many psychiatrists accuse their colleagues in the Association of "caving in under political pressure," without sufficient research or scientific evidence to justify such a change. The results of a 1977 poll of psychiatrists, published in *Medical Aspects of Human Sexuality*, indicated 69 percent still believe homosexuality to be pathological (a sickness), 13 percent were undecided.

Space will not permit the recitation of other signs of homosexual militancy—homosexual marriages, judges who award adoption of boys to known homosexuals, the San Francisco School Board approval of the inclusion of homosexuality taught in the sex education classes as "gay" rather than deviant behavior. But that isn't the nightmare promised by H. R. 2998 (co-sponsored by twenty-five members of the U.S. House of Representatives and authored by Rep. Ed Koch) or H.R. 5239. Under these bills, all public schools will be required to hire homosexuals—and Congressman Koch has since been elected mayor of New York! One of his first executive orders after taking office was to strike down all sexual discrimination laws in hiring city employees. This was immediately opposed by the New York City fire chief.

Now do you understand why militant homosexuals hate Anita Bryant so? They suffered their only defeat at the hands of Christians who rallied to the leadership and the cry of "Save Our Children." The homosexuals had come up with a program that was so blatantly evil that on June 17, 1977, 202,319 voters (69.3 percent) called for the repeal of the Dade County ordinance that forbade even Christian schools from excluding homosexual teachers. As Miss Bryant declared afterward, "The people of Dade County—the normal majority—have said, 'Enough! Enough! Enough!' They have voted to repeal an obnoxious assault on our moral values despite our community's reputation as one of the most liberal areas in the nation. All America and all the world will hear what the people have said."[34]

The Aftermath

Howls of protest resounded from homosexuals, bleeding heart liberals, and the news media throughout the nation. As one leading weekly magazine wailed, "Americans have not quite matured sufficiently to permit others their own personal sexual preference." They missed the whole point! Americans haven't "matured" enough to permit perverts to teach our children that deviant sexual behavior is a normal way of life.

Homosexual rallies and demonstrations took place all over the nation. *Time* magazine told of a special meeting in New York City where twenty-eight leaders of homosexual organizations gathered to plan an attack. They declared war on Anita Bryant. Wherever she appeared she was to be picketed. To date their pressure on her has not let up.

When they discovered that Tom Brokaw was to interview her live on the "Today Show," they threatened to bring the city to a standstill by putting 10,000 demonstrators on the street—with one day's notice. So the network flew her in secretly and pretaped the interview (which I thought was atypical for Mr. Brokaw and frankly, I was disappointed he was so nasty to her).

So far our "born-again" President has not invited the "born-again" heroine of Dade County to the White House to commend her moral and spiritual courage. But while he was out of town, Midge Constanza, one of his advisers, entertained fourteen militant lesbians (the first time such a meeting has occurred in the White House), allowing them to air their grievances. As they were leaving, one of them remarked that Ms. Constanza had used her office as "a door opener." We hope the door is not opened too far.

The New Gay Alliance

The New Alliance for Gay Equality (the New A.G.E.) is the latest organization of the militant homosexuals. Apparently the homosexual movement realizes that the tide of public opinion is going against them (the thought that they have gone too far hasn't seemed to occur to them yet), and they can't afford another defeat, particularly in California, where the next big legal battle will be fought.

California Senator John Briggs, a father and former businessman, so strongly resented homosexuals moving into Dade County to fight Anita Bryant that he and his wife flew there to help out. Mrs. Briggs proved particularly useful since she speaks fluent Spanish. Both Senator Briggs and his wife found it to be a deeply spiritual experience. He re-dedicated his life to Christ and she was "born again." I have met them both several times since and can testify that they are changed people.

Senator Briggs has filed an initiative petition to the California Constitution, bringing to the voters this matter of forbidding known homosexuals to be school teachers of the young, which seems to be the bottom line issue today. Do the rights of the straight 95 percent have to be violated to protect the rights of the 5 percent? Or stated another way, does a straight parent have the right to protect his children from being exposed to a homosexual teacher in the tax-supported schoolhouse? The Briggs initiative does not discriminate

against homosexuals, but it does protect school children from
being taught perverted sex by a homosexual.

The New A.G.E. has supposedly been endorsed in a
fund-raising appeal by several big names in Hollywood (some
of whom vigorously opposed the Viet Nam war, and one of
whom even went to North Viet Nam and condemned our
P.O.W.'s for their "aggression"). The New A.G.E. plans a
"massive professional media outreach to educate the public"
in opposing the initiative. "A benefit concert will be held
in the future." We can only lament that their "benefit" is not
for California's school children instead of *against* them. The
outcome will not merely affect California school children but
will become a barometer of how much perversion is too much.
If the Christian community gets off their pews, digs down into
their pockets, and supports this initiative, the onrush of
homosexuality can be stopped throughout the country. If it
isn't halted in California, our nation will take another giant
step toward the death of our culture.

The Militant Future

"Homosexual rights are going to be the
civil rights issue of the 1980s," declared
Jean O'Leary, the militant homosexual
appointed by President Jimmy Carter to the
National Committee for the Observance
of International Women's Year. This is the
first time that a publicly acknowledged
homosexual has ever been appointed to a
high federal position.[35]

Miss O'Leary's prediction is quite sobering in view of the
fact that homosexuality has gone militant even before the '80s
arrive. Organized, experienced, determined (some would say
obsessed), and well-financed homosexuals have infiltrated
key positions of influence in government, media, writing,
Hollywood, and education. The battle lines are drawn as never
before for the moral contest of the century.

We have experienced a few victories against their advance, among them an enormous increase in the drinking of Florida orange juice (in spite of the homosexual boycotts), so that sales have skyrocketed and orange juice stocks dramatically increased, causing the Florida Citrus Commission to renew Anita Bryant's advertising contract. But the homosexuals won't give up! They are out to force the acceptance of their deviant behavior as normal and the creation of a climate conducive to recruitment. Let us hope that straights will wake up to the fact that while they are drinking orange juice, the homosexual community, by militance and secret political maneuvering, is designing a program to increase the tidal wave of homosexuality that will drown our children in a polluted sea of sexual perversion—and will eventually destroy America as it did Rome, Greece, Pompeii, and Sodom.

Note from the author: Anita Bryant and the Christians of Dade County touched a hidden nerve in the hearts of millions of Americans, for since their victory in Florida, three other cities have overwhelmingly voted the same way: St. Paul, Minnesota, Wichita, Kansas (by a vote of 4 to 1), and Eugene, Oregon. Let us hope they have started a landslide that will blanket the nation. In addition, the U.S. Supreme Court refused to hear a case filed by a homosexual teacher in Oregon for being fired because of his sexual preference. Experts interpret that to mean that it is constitutional for school boards to protect their students from sexually deviant teachers.

Just six days before this book went to press, the United Presbyterian Church, in their well-publicized annual session in San Diego, voted down a commission recommendation to ordain self-acknowledged homosexuals into the gospel ministry. This came just one week after State Senator John Briggs filed his initiative petition to the California constitution that enables school boards to fire homosexual teachers. With 150,000 signatures more than the required 338,000, it seems certain the voters of California will also have an opportunity to express themselves in the November election.

Even though the tide is turning against legalizing homosexuality, you can be sure of one thing—they will not give up!

The Church of Sodom

"An evangelical church for homosexuals? You've got to be kidding!" That was my reaction to the news that a defrocked Pentecostal minister, Troy Perry, announced he was founding a homosexual church in Los Angeles called "The Metropolitan Community Church." Twelve people showed up for the first service; nine were Perry's personal friends and three responded to his ad in a local homosexual tabloid. Who would have believed that in less than ten years his "church" would grow to a local congregation of almost one thousand and serve as the mother for a homosexual denomination of 67,000, meeting in 110 churches and missions around the world?

Converts to this church, which claims to be "evangelical," came largely from straight churches rather than from the secular homosexual community. Those whose guilt-ridden consciences made them uncomfortable in Bible-believing churches because of clear teaching on homosexuality as sin became ready converts to the Metropolitan teachings that approve sodomy, which the Bible calls "abomination." *Newsweek* magazine indicated that 40 percent of his parishioners came from Catholic churches and 40 percent from evangelical Protestantism.

According to a very candid interview published in the

September 1973 issue of *Playboy*, Troy Perry attended a fundamental Bible school, switched to Pentecostalism, was ordained at nineteen, and married a minister's daughter, who bore him two children. Like many other self-deceived homosexuals, he read the writings of a humanist thinker and deduced, "I'm gay! I've always been gay." He then admits to "fantasizing" about men when he was only five, having his first homosexual experience at age nine, and engaging in gang masturbatory escapades at church camp. Advised that marriage would "straighten him out," he pledged his "faithfulness" to a trusting young Christian woman and promised "till death us do part" in the typical ceremony. Unfortunately, he found, according to the article, that five minutes after "the act of marriage" he was left feeling that "something was lacking." Within six months he acknowledged having an experience with another male which left him "completely satisfied."

For three and one-half years Perry fought an inner battle to go straight, but to no avail. While visiting in California, he looked through some "physique" magazines that "excited" him. He purchased several of the magazines, and "they turned him on." He read a paperback book on homosexuality and determined "beyond a shadow of a doubt" that he was a homosexual. Finally he and his wife separated, and she took the children back to live with her parents. He proceeded to identify with the gay community and, according to Dr. Walter Martin, who claims to have been his Bible teacher in prehomosexual days, said he lived with a "lover" for some time but finally was jilted. In the midst of the depression that so often plagues the sensitive, love-starved homosexual after breaking up with his male partner, he almost took his own life. Now he would have us believe that God has led him to start a denomination for Christian homosexuals!

The Leading
of God

It has long been interesting to me that people can claim to violate the principles of God in their personal lives and then without repentance expect the Christian community to follow them as they further disobey the clear teachings of Scripture. In this case they want to call "righteous" that which God labels "unrighteous."

One thing you can write clearly on the action level of your brain: God will *never* lead a person into anything that is forbidden in his Word. That would make God contradict himself, for he inspired the writing of the Bible. In fact, one of the tests of a spirit's leadership is whether it leads in accord with the Word of God; if it doesn't, it is an impostor spirit.

The churches of Sodom are spreading to major cities throughout the U.S., Canada, and Europe. The Metropolitan Community Church denomination is even sending "missionaries" out to organize new churches for homosexuals. Most of these "churches," taking their cue from Troy Perry, encourage their members to live with and marry members of their own sex. One of their goals is to provide a place where homosexuals can worship God, not as outcasts and lepers, but as children of God. As my pastor-friend John MacArthur has said, "You might as well have churches for fornicators, adulterers, murderers, and robbers."

The success of the Metropolitan Community Church has inspired similar Roman Catholic congregations to spring up, along with liberal groups and, in some cities, synagogues. If the next decade experiences the growth level of the past ten years, religious homosexuals will turn into an epidemic.

A Visit to the
Church of Sodom

I wanted to observe a Metropolitan Church in action
personally before writing this chapter. My wife and I attended
the local congregation on a Sunday morning, and I must say
it was the most unusual service I have ever attended. Wearing
our usual Sunday attire, we stuck out like sore thumbs in a
congregation of about 125. Evidently we unnerved some, for
they hardly know how to greet us. They were neither friendly
nor unfriendly. The service was very casual. A choir, led by a
guitarist, sang the usual mindless songs of the permissive
culture. There was no doctrine, Bible teaching, or mention of
Christ in any of them—just the mournful wail of "luv, luv,
luv." Don't misunderstand, I am all for "love," but love for
God *first*. That is the first commandment in both the Old
and New Testaments. Like most movements based on
erroneous teachings, the homosexual church has developed a
man-centered theology instead of a God-centered doctrine.
What they don't realize is that man functions best when
obedient to God, not when he worships man and his desires
or feelings.

The one female in the choir really grieved my wife and me.
An attractive young woman dressed like a man in cords
and shirt, she was obviously doing everything she could to
appear mannish. With both hands in her back pockets,
she sang pleasantly while attempting to imitate a sex she did
not possess. I couldn't help thinking about the emptiness,
loneliness, and lack of fulfillment which lay ahead of her
if she pursued the unhappy gay life.

The most uncomfortable part of the service for me pertained
to the open expressions of affection between members of the
same sex, the like of which I have never seen in church, even
among uninhibited teen-agers of the opposite sex. My wife
and I watched a blonde woman in front of us blowing into the

ear of the dark-haired woman at her side and nibbling at her
earlobe until she had the woman trembling. Two rows further
up, the two men who had walked in holding hands sat
snuggled up, one with his arm around the other. Eventually
one ran his hand into the other's shirt and fondled his chest—
during the sermon. Several "lovers" in the audience seemed
bent on showing their affection (or possession) in some
physical manner—far more so than that indulged in by the
average "straight" audience. For the first quarter of the
service a woman in the third row kept looking back anxiously
toward the door. Finally another woman came in, and as she
slid into her seat, they kissed warmly on the mouth.

It was amazing to me that this little church had three
ministers, all avowed homosexuals and all formally dressed in
clerical garb. The preacher was extremely personable and
articulate, but I found his definition of sin rather interesting.
It had nothing to do with disobeying God or his Word but only
with offending man. "Sin is alienation from others," he
explained and proceeded to state that anything you do that
alienates another is sin. Interestingly enough, he gave no
Scripture to prove his thesis, but then, little he said was related
to the Bible.

To us the most startling part of the service occurred at the
beginning when the preacher first stepped into the pulpit.
Calling attention to the altar, he announced, "Our lovely altar
flowers today were given by Larry and Bill to commemorate
this first anniversary of their meeting. It was one year ago
they met here in our church." I thought, "Shades of Sodom
and Gomorrah! What must God think of two sodomists
commemorating the anniversary of their relationship by
desecrating an altar with flowers." It certainly doesn't
exonerate them of their sin. The tragedy is, they can be
expected to do something like that when the "shepherd" calls
sodomy "love" and, when pretending to speak for God, he
says, "All love is good."

After a well-delivered, humorous message, the preacher invited the audience to pray before he served the Lord's Supper. We chose that opportunity to exit discreetly. As we tiptoed past the two ushers in the back, I couldn't help observing them with heads bowed, holding hands. (Somehow it didn't seem to take on the same significance as when the Denver Broncos hold hands in the huddle on a third down and short yardage play.)

The church of Sodom (or of your city) may do some good for certain individuals and may even bring a few unhappy gays out of their miseries to faith in Christ, but it won't call them from their sin. It is bad enough for a society in general (and homosexuals in particular) to hear a militant homosexual or professional school teacher extol the blessings of homosexuality. It is much worse to hear or see an ordained minister, who claims to believe the Bible, advocate such a life style. There is no question in my mind that the damage done by the church of Sodom to the Kingdom of God and our culture will be far greater than any conceivable good it may produce. The following are some of the harmful results of this "church."

1. It will encourage many thousands to enter the unhappy gay life style by deceiving them into thinking that they have received a Christian endorsement. (As they say in their literature, "Board members and consultants include some of *the most respected evangelicals* in America today." The truth is, no respected known evangelical endorses this movement; they are only sodomists claiming to be evangelicals.)

2. It will hinder many unhappy gays from leaving this sinful life style by leading them to believe they can be both practicing Christians and practicing homosexuals. The last thing any sinner needs is ministerial endorsement of his sin.

3. It will encourage many fathers and some mothers who are presently bisexual to abandon their families as some of the church leaders have done, leaving a trail of heartbroken loved

ones while they selfishly satisfy their own fleshly lusts. The
Bible teaches that Christian leaders should "be an example
to the believers." A far better example is for a bisexual
married person to face the fact that a same-sex liaison is sin
and to "flee from it" for the Lord's sake, fulfilling his
responsibilities to God and his partner as a husband and father.

4. It will contribute to the decline of our culture by giving
a deceptively Christian approval to a perverted life style. This
will confuse some Christian voters and many non-Christians
into thinking that Christians are divided on homosexuality,
even encouraging citizens to vote in favor of loosening laws
against homosexuality at a time when they need
strengthening. Every issue which requires legal action finds
the homosexual movement using liberal or self-deceived
homosexual ministers to encourage Christians to favor lenient
laws on homosexuality—contrary to the Word of God.

5. It will give credence to the lie that "they can't help it,"
"God made them this way," or as one said, "Am I to blame
because the Almighty slipped a cog in creation?" This
blasphemous suggestion that God made a person homosexual
is particularly dangerous. It has often been said, "If you tell a
lie often enough, people will eventually believe it is the
truth." They will believe the lie sooner if a "clergyman"
tells it.

God would never have commanded the death penalty for
homosexuality if a person was really "born that way." All
capital punishment was for crimes a person committed
voluntarily. Homosexuality is no exception (Leviticus 20).

The Dangers of a Homosexual Society

All signs indicate that we are rushing into a homosexually lenient society. Unless the sleeping majority bestirs itself, the media, militants, misguided educators, and politicians will strike down every moral law that has historically kept the miseries of the unhappy gay life limited to 4 or 5 percent of our population. In the name of "civil rights," "human rights," "individual rights," and "freedom," they are creating a danger far greater than they realize.

As a Christian, I do not wish to add to the unhappy gay community more trouble than they already have created for themselves. Nor do I wish to instigate a hysterical reaction to them as individuals. As God knows my heart, I love them and pray for their release from this sin and the resultant eventual destruction of their souls. But I would be less than fair if I did not call attention to the many dangers that accepting their sexual habits as normal behavior will produce in our Judeo-Christian culture. The following dangers are selected in a descending order, beginning with the greatest.

1. It will at least double the homosexual community in the next decade.

Every country and civilization that has endorsed

189

homosexuality as an optional life style has seen an increase in homosexuality, England is a good example. Since the laws against homosexuality were struck down by the British House of Lords in 1957, England's homosexual population has mushroomed. Marriage has declined, and births, of course, have dropped off. In spite of homosexual leaders' assurance to the contrary, relaxing homosexual laws will not decrease interest in it, but will increase the curiosity level of young people prior to puberty, at the time they are naturally hero worshipers. The fact that their sex drive at that age may be inclined toward same-sex expression does not make it right. Instead, it makes it harmful, for as we have seen, it tends to entrench the habit in a young man's life before his natural sex drive is ignited, thus nullifying his heterosexual potential. Whatever we as a society can do to keep innocent young lads, who would otherwise grow up to be heterosexual, from learning to be homosexual early in life, the better off they and our society will be.

Unfortunately, we cannot give the unhappy gays the acceptance they demand without sentencing millions of innocent youths to a lifetime of this misery. That is a price too great to pay! It violates the moral standards of God, runs contrary to the good of our country, and is in opposition to the best interests of our youth. Therefore, we must not give in to the selfish demands of the homosexual community.

Learn a lesson from history. During Prohibition our fathers were told, "Legalize drinking and people won't drink as much." Today one out of ten of our fellow citizens is an alcoholic. The past generation was warned not to discipline their children lest their creativity be inhibited. Today we have an undisciplined generation with an inordinate percentage of rebellious adults living below their potential. In the late '60s I fought against radical inflammatory sex education in the public schools because I knew what would happen. Educators insisted that young people needed to know all about sex.

Today the "know all's" have flooded our society with promiscuity, venereal disease, unwed mothers, and a divorce rate more than double what it was ten years ago. We can anticipate the same with homosexuality if we do away with our present laws.

Why is it that twentieth-century man considers himself so intelligent that he can overturn moral and cultural codes that have formed our civilization's bulwark for centuries? These disciples of "change for change's sake" are nothing but inexperienced social experimenters, with humanity's happiness hanging in the balance. Admittedly, there are millions of unhappy gays in our society. But striking down all laws and restrictions which govern them and accepting their sexual preference as normal instead of perverted is too big a risk to take. Besides, rejection by a straight society isn't the cause of their miseries; their miserable life style produces its own anguish. The insecurities of love relationships won't change. The lack of a deep family tie won't change. And the fear of growing old and undesirable won't change. They are an inseparable part of the unhappy gay life style. It would be cruel and heartless for our society to destroy laws that keep it from becoming contagious.

Not only Christian leaders and counselors but an increasing number of psychiatrists are alarmed about the situation.

Dr. Van Ferney, a member of the psychiatric staff at New Jersey's Medical Center in Princeton, urged parents to fight.

In an interview with *National Enquirer* reporter Maury M. Breecher, published June 7, 1977, Dr. Van Ferney said that

> constant media coverage of the gays has made their lifestyle appear to be commonplace and acceptable rather than unusual and deviant. This is particularly disturbing to those who are concerned that their children could easily be misled into thinking that homosexuality is an attractive kind of lifestyle to adopt.

> Parents are absolutely correct to be
> fearful of the effects all of this is having on
> their kids. Homosexuals are so active on
> high school and college campuses that there
> is hardly a child in America who has not
> been exposed to their influence.
>
> You have a right to raise decent children
> in a decent society. But that right will be
> taken away from you unless you make
> yourself heard. If parents capitulate to the
> homosexual influences which surround
> them, society as we know it will be
> destroyed.

Two other psychiatrists quoted in the same article
expressed similar views.

Dr. Samuel Silverman, associate professor of psychiatry
at Harvard Medical School, was quoted as saying:

> I would also advise parents to protest
> vigorously if any of their children's teachers
> are professed homosexuals.
>
> It's very admirable to be tolerant and
> sensitive to people's civil rights—but you
> have to draw the line somewhere, and a
> homosexual teacher who flaunts his sexual
> aberrations publicly is as dangerous to
> children as one of the religious cultists.
>
> Homosexuals have not only come out of
> the closet, they have become militant.
> They are demanding all kinds of "rights"
> ... to be fully accepted as "normal," to
> be able to marry, to adopt and raise children
> and to have their lifestyle presented as a
> perfectly normal alternative to
> heterosexuality.
>
> Many of these militant gays are not
> fighting for their own civil rights but are
> attempting to win converts to their way
> of life.

And Dr. Silverman added: *"What is really needed now is
a ground-roots movement against these militants."*

Dr. Charles W. Socarides, clinical professor of psychiatry

at the State University of New York and a leading authority
on the treatment of homosexuality, warned:

> There's no doubt in my mind that if
> homosexuality is further normalized and
> raised to a level of complete social
> acceptability, there will be a tremendous
> rise in the incidence of homosexuality. It
> would have dire effects for society.
> Homosexuality militates against the family,
> drives the sexes in opposite directions
> and neglects the child's growth and sexual
> identity.[36]

2. It will increase the recruitment of children and young
people into homosexuality. Most homosexuals are quick to
claim that the majority of their number *do not* molest children
or try to recruit them to a life of homosexuality, and they may
be right. In fairness to them, I know homosexuals who get
irate at "chicken hawks" who prey on young people and
children. Nevertheless, many homosexuals (and police
officials indicate that their number is increasing at an alarming
rate) make it their business to recruit. As I have said before,
if some homosexuals didn't recruit, they would become
extinct because they do not propagate.

Not all homosexuals use force in their recruitment tactics.
Some lure boys by the offer of friendship, drugs, money,
clothes, travel, or whatever the child responds to. But whether
we like it or not, unknown to many today there is a male (ages
ten to sixteen) recruitment program going on that has raised
male prostitution to alarming proportions. One police officer
reports that there are five male prostitutes on the streets of his
city for every hooker. That makes recruitment not only
pleasurable but profitable—a time-tested formula for
increasing anything.

My files are loaded with clippings verifying the increase
in recruitment efforts; it is impossible to include them all.
Reproduced on the next page are some samples showing

Ex-teachers indicted for lewd acts with boys

By PAUL LEAVITT
Register Staff Writer

Two former Ankeny school teachers were indicted Tuesday by the Polk County Grand Jury on multiple charges of engaging in lascivious acts with boys under the age of 16.

Robert Novak, 31, a junior high school social studies teacher, was named in a 13-count indictment alleging that between January, 1975 and January, 1977, he did "fondle or touch" the genitals of 11 boys.

John W. Buck, 25, a high school music teacher, was accused in a eight-count indictment alleging that he committed the same offense eight boys during the period June 1974, to November, 1976.

 JACK ROBERTS

Homosexuals: the ugly side

"They call themselves 'chicken hawks' and they openly advertise in magazines for 'chickens,'" said Coral Gables Police Sgt. Tony Raimondo. "The 'hawks' are grown men ... homosexuals. The 'chickens are boys, ages 10 to 14. The 'hawks' want the 'chickens' for sex. The 'hawks' take pictures of themselves with the 'chickens' and pass them around. It is a disgusting business."

Raimondo said that in the course of an investigation which started

Refusal of Gays' Ad By Newspaper Stands

WASHINGTON — (AP) — The Supreme Court Monday refused to consider whether the editor of a student newspaper at a state university may refuse a paid advertisement describing counseling and legal services offered by an alliance for homosexuals.

The justices let stand a U.S. Circuit Court decision upholding the student editor's right to reject the

its editors reject. "Compulsion to publish is unconstitutional," the high court said in that case.

But the ACLU attorneys argued that this case is different because the student newspaper is published by a state institution.

A three-judge panel of the circuit court in New Orleans split 2-1 on the case.

Teacher Faces Abuse Rap

By BOB KAPPSTATTER

A popular 30-year-old English teacher at a Brooklyn junior high school for talented children was charged yesterday with sexually abusing several young boys in his classes.

said the incidents, which light only recently, occurred at k Twain JHS at 2401 Neptune ey Island.

allegedly were "sexually fondled" by the teacher in his classroom during private conferences.

The teacher, Lawrence Gambelli, was arrested at his Bensonhurst home, where he lives with his invalid mother. Gambelli, described as "well liked by everyone," denied the charges.

Gambelli was charged

NEWS BRIEFS

OC Teacher Held On Sex Charges

ORANGE — Orange High School's band director has be arrested and booked into Orange County Jail on suspicion of perversion plus child molesting and annoyance, a jail spokesm

Greg Wendell Isbell, 28, of Orange, Monday was charged wi 10 counts of oral copulation and one count of child molesting a annoyance The charges involve boys under the age of 18, sa deputy Dist Atty Mel Jensen.

Orange High School principal Jack Fox said the school i opened an investigation after receiving complaints from p '— boys have been identified as being involv

Why a 13-year-old is selling his body

Boys are selling themselves not only on the streets of New York, Los Angeles, San Francisco, Philadelphia, Chicago, Baltimore and New Orleans, but also in smaller cities across the country: Waukesha, Wis.; Santa Clara, Cal.; Laredo, Texas and in even smaller towns.

In street jargon, the boys are known as chickens; their customers as chickenhawks. In the major cities, young male hookers wander through the streets in search of customers while call-boy operations flourish.

Pimps, skilled in initiating young

Teacher Accused of Sex Acts With Boy Students

BY LEE HARRIS
Times Staff Writer

A 34-year-old bachelor Los Angeles elementary schoolteacher was arraigned Monday on 16 felony counts involving alleged sexual relations with at least six of his present former boy students.

le is Gary Paul Letherer, a fourth- _e teacher at the Toland Elemen-_ _School in the Glassell Park area_ Eagle Rock.

he victims, according to northeast _tion ___ John Sack_ ranged in age

instruction and taught wrestling after school, police said.

The investigation began last week after the mother of one young boy grew suspicious about her son's apparent emotional distress and quizzed him. The child finally told her about a sexual contact with the teacher, officers said.

Letherer was arrested Tuesday after school and booked in connection with that case

By law   Berman said, five
4 sites

Former scoutmaster convicted of homosexual acts with boys

BLOUNTVILLE (AP) — The scoutmaster of a Boy Scout troop was sentenced to 30 to 46 years in prison Tuesday after being found guilty of committing homosexual acts with six boys during an overnight campout last summer.

The verdict was returned against Jacob M. Bethany, 36. Kingsport, following a two-day trial in which the six youths testified that Bethany performed various ___

returning the verdict on six charges of performing acts against nature. Earlier, the defense rested its case without calling a single witness.

Bethany, a water works employee, was sentenced by Judge Edgar Calhoun. The sentence represents consecutive terms of 10 to 15 years on three of the six charges and ___ ___ on the

Bethany to h___ during an o__ State Park r_ trial indictm_

Another camping th sex with h Bethany

4 Men Accused Of Abusing Boys

FLINT — (AP) — Four Flint men have been charged with engaging more than 30 boys in oral copulation, sodomy and photography sessions of sex acts, the Genesee County Prosecutor's Office announced.

Three of the men have been arre___ degree and third-degree ___

charges of first-___ duct. Prosecutor being sought on _ t 14.
d to uncover an _ knew each ___ ther men.

Police find sexually abused children

LOS ANGELES (UPI) — Police estimate there are 30,000 sexually abused children in Los Angeles mostly young boys used by homosexuals, including $1,000-a-day prostitutes aged 12.

"This is not just a Los Angeles problem, although it is becoming more prevalent here," said Riddle

"It's like a contagious disease and it's spreading all over the country."

Investigations have turned up rings that supply boys to adult males he said, with links throughout the country, including reports of private clubs and "an interstate network of 'houses' set up like private _____ to provide 'cadets' for

vestigation, his division's Abused Child Unit is being strengthened, Riddle said.

"This is not being done to harass homosexuals. It's being done to protect the juveniles."

The preliminary ivestigation indicated, by "street estimate, that there are about 25,000 boys between 14 and 17 being used by about 15,000 homosexual

men were arrested, warrants were obtained for two others and 44 criminal charges filed, he said, including child endangering, contributing narcotics to minors and sexual offenses. The investigators took into custody 17 boys, 11 of them under 15.

Sgt. Jackie Howell, head of the Child Abuse Unit, ____ the typical youth as

from a broken or neglected home with no father figure, living on the streets and starved for love.

The boys often trade sex for money and drugs, primarily marijuana and pills, she said.

From there, they are moved into posing for pornographic photos and roles in "chicken films." 8mm and 16mm movies which sell for $100 a reel and ___

Homosexuals used Scout troop

NEW ORLEANS AP — Seventeen men have been charged in a widening investigation of the use of a Boy Scout troop here to supply boys for homosexual acts

It has been like dropping a pebble into water," said District Attorney Harry Connick "You think you've got it all but the ripple ring keeps spreading

The men were charged with perform-

ing sex acts with boys aged 8 to 16 over a two-year period ending last September. Not all of the scouts in the now defunct troop were involved.

We find some of the men have also been active in other parts of the country," Connick added. "Some have been prosecuted in England and the Philippines for sex involving children."

The first of a series of trials was

scheduled in Criminal District Court on Tuesday but a lawyer for Raymond Woodall, 38, of New Orleans asked for a delay He said Woodall had been committed to a state mental hospital due to severe depression and suicidal tendencies.

Woodall, assistant scoutmaster of Boy Scout Troop 137, was charged with 13 counts of "unnatural carnal knowledge."

The most numerous charges we against Richard Jacobs of Ar Mass., a Boston suburb, and Halvorsen, who was troop sco

Jacobs, whose trial is sch 30, is charged with 13 c gravated crime against carries a maximum p per count.

headlines. The following are just a few abbreviated excerpts.

.. 35,000 boys were molested in Los
Angeles alone last year, 25,000 of them
under 18,

, , , A Los Angeles police captain said,
"A six-week investigation revealed that
thousands of youthful victims are being
subjected to every conceivable sex crime,
including acts of sadomasochism (inflicted
pain for sexual gratification). More than
25,000 juveniles under 17 years of age are
used sexually by approximately 15,000
adult males. Pornographic materials are
used to stimulate them sexually, and
narcotics are used to lower their inhibitions.
A 12-year-old boy can earn $1,000 a day,
most of which goes to a pimp."

, . . Two groups operating out of Los
Angeles are apparently finding a ready
market for young Mexican boys . , . One or
two adults will drive to any one of the
California-Mexico border towns and
recruit four youngsters for a trip to Los
Angeles. Before leaving Mexico, the boys
are scrubbed clean and dressed in
nearly-new clothes to make them look as
Mexican-American as possible. Getting
them across the border into the United
States is a comparatively simple matter
as evidenced by the fact that California
now houses close to a million illegal aliens.
Once the boys arrive in Los Angeles, they
are distributed to anxiously waiting
customers. When they have made the
circuit, they are driven back to Mexico and
replaced by fresh recruits. Police files
show that one Los Angeles school teacher
spent a considerable amount of time
bringing groups of boys aged seven through
thirteen across the border every three
months, using the city Hermosillo as his
source. He has since discontinued the
operation and voluntarily entered a private
institution for treatment,

. . . Another story tells of a man who

searched for days for a missing 16-year-old
and finally located him in a sleazy hotel
semiconscious from heroin, lying face
down on a dirty bed. His "provider" had
several men waiting in the hall to use
him for ten dollars apiece. One of those
who had finished with him had previously
contracted gonorrhea.

From New York to Miami, from Dallas to San Diego come
repeated reports of those caught attempting to "recruit,"
entice, or molest the young. And remember, homosexuality
isn't respected or considered a "civil right" yet. Can you
imagine what America will be like if it ever is?

A study of 1800 students at U. C. Berkeley revealed that
500 had been solicited by homosexuals, 300 of these before
they were sixteen years of age. If homosexuality becomes
fashionable, no one will be immune.

3. Leniency toward homosexuality will endanger the civil
rights of the majority.

If the 1977 version of the "Gay Rights" legislation
introduced into Congress earlier this year by the present mayor
of New York is passed, it will come at the expense of the civil
rights of the majority. You will not be able to refuse to rent
your home to mating homosexuals, even if your straight
children are being raised next door. Straight employers will
not be able to hire only straights; that freedom will be gone.
"Big Brother" from Washington can insist that you maintain
a homosexual job quota when hiring. In fact, you may have
to dismiss some straight employees to make room for
unhappy gays on your staff. It is conceivable that Christian
colleges' approval for veterans benefits will be jeopardized
unless they hire a certain number of homosexuals and lesbians
(probably one out of ten). And worst of all, as a straight
taxpayer you could not object if your son or daughter happens
to draw a homosexual teacher. Your only recourse would
be to enroll your child in a Christian school.

Admittedly, some homosexual teachers are serving in public schools today, and many are probably good teachers. But as long as it is illegal to do so, they cannot flaunt their homosexuality. When all job discrimination for homosexuality is removed (and it will be if the silent majority remains silent), teachers can be expected to brainwash our children with the "blessings" of the unhappy gay life. Misery loves company, and you can expect homosexual teachers single-handedly to double the homosexual community within ten years, not by recruiting, but by preparing youngsters mentally for the recruiters. Let us pray it will never come to that! If it does, in my opinion our society is lost. Permitting homosexuals to orient young, impressionable minds toward homosexuality will be the bottom line in our culture. When we cross that line, I believe we will have descended to the ultimate in abominations.

The school classroom is a privileged sanctuary where teachers are entrusted—by parents—with the minds of young people and children. Such a sanctuary should reflect the moral standards of the community. It was never meant to be a gigantic social laboratory for experimentation at taxpayers' expense. At one time parents had some control over the moral training within the schools, but ever since federal aid to education was approved, the control of the schools has been taken over by the social experimenters of Washington. Now the only option for a parent who does not approve of the moral teaching his children are receiving is to put them in a private Christian school—if he can afford it. Otherwise, his children may be subject (depending on the standards and courage of the local principal) to every immoral concept except one: homosexuality. Although parental complaints are voiced occasionally, many sex education teachers get by with ridiculing virtue, morals, and chastity while promoting "free love," "experimentation," and "promiscuity." We have placed only one prohibition upon teachers: they cannot

endorse homosexuality. Some sex education courses
(according to *Time* magazine, September 8, 1975) are already
being written with the idea that "Gay Is Good." One gay task
force of the American Library Association has already begun
such a campaign, anticipating the passage of this "gay right"
—that is, that gays can teach school without threat of losing
their jobs. If that day comes, the public schools and libraries
will be flooded with pro-homosexual literature that will
subvert the sex direction of millions of today's children and
young people.

We should learn a lesson from gay college professors.
The lenient attitude of many college administrators is
appalling in this regard. They often make no attempt to
fire known homosexuals from their faculty. Only when the
issue is publicly paraded and condemned do they take action
and then reluctantly, blaming the "backward notions of the
ignorant masses" for not understanding those creative people.
I have had college young people tell me that homosexual
teachers make no real attempt to hide their sexual preference
and often go out of their way to subtly exalt it—all the time
watching for those young men who seem to respond. These he
can invite to his home for "special tutoring." One student
told of a vile pro-homosexual film he was subjected to in
class, after which the teacher announced that he was showing
another, which was "more explicit," at his bachelor
apartment that night. Since the administration frowned on a
screening in class, a private showing was the only other option
available to the teacher. The "extra credit" film was offered
on a voluntary basis. Yes, Virginia, recruiting is being
undertaken by today's college teachers, whether we like to
admit it or not.

What Americans will tolerate on our college campuses
among "adult" young people, they will not yet authorize in
high school and below. Fearing a community outcry,
homosexual elementary and secondary teachers keep their

sexual preference to themselves, and very few have been found recruiting. But the minute the gay rights bill passes, they will come out of their school closets, propagandizing, brainwashing, and indoctrinating our youth, and an increased number will begin brazenly to entice, recruit, and in some cases even molest.

Present trends are such that it is only a matter of time before the taxpaying majority will be overpowered by legislation to provide the homosexual minority the right to ''do their own thing''! However, we can't have it both ways. That is, if we grant minority rights to the homosexuals, we cannot retain majority rights of straights to protect their children from homosexual exaltation and indoctrination. Either we continue our centuries-old tradition of majority rights or we abolish it for a new ''gay rights'' law. A better title than ''gay rights'' would be ''abomination of desolations.''

Everyone Discriminates

The media and educators have become paranoid about the subject of discrimination, carrying their position to illogical extremes. While we do not believe in racial discrimination, we do maintain sexual discrimination. A vast majority of Americans (95 percent) believe that heterosexuality is normal and homosexuality is abnormal. The majority do not oppose the minority's right to live and work in our country, but we do contend that they cannot teach our young, and most would insist that they should not be entrusted with enforcing our laws. There is nothing evil or un-American about that—it is honorable and fair. But if we fail to stand up and defend our position, we will be defrauded of our majority rights by a loud, militant, and overinfluential minority.

4. A homosexually lenient society will cause an increase in crimes and sadistic murders.

At the risk of alienating the many law-abiding homosexuals who would never purposely harm another human being, it must be pointed out that a much higher crime potential and tendency toward sadistic violence exists among homosexuals than among straights. Throughout my interviews with police officers from San Diego to San Francisco, the only one who questioned the fact that homosexuals have a much higher ratio of violence was himself a homosexual. He refuses to face the fact that if less than 10 percent of the population is homosexual, then only 10 percent of the violent crimes should have been committed by homosexuals. Those I questioned indicated that although sexual preference of criminals is not usually recorded, even the number of those who can be confirmed as being homosexuals is much higher than 10 percent.

While writing this book, I have been appalled by the number of sadistic crimes attributed to homosexuals. The famous trash-can murderer (at least twenty-four deaths)* confessed to several homicides and received a life sentence. A porno film maker of lesbian movies was apprehended for murdering his actresses, and a shocking revelation was made in Boston recently when seventeen prominent men (including a child psychiatrist and a school administrator) were arrested in a nationwide "homosexual prostitution ring involving boys."

It is difficult for straight citizens to accept the extreme measures some homosexuals will use to get their own way (particularly militants). *Time* magazine on August 29, 1977, reported the experience of Adam Walinsky, who had written an article which questioned a special law protective of homosexuals. About fifty gays attacked his house. "They cut the telephone lines, pelted the house with eggs, set off firecrackers, and chanted through bullhorns, 'Walinsky, you

---

*A January 9, 1978, Los Angeles *Herald Examiner* news story indicates they now claim there were thirty-two trash-can victims.

liar, we'll set your house on fire' . . . He then asked, 'Why do people who claim to want human rights go around like a bunch of storm troopers trying to intimidate others from expressing their views?' ''

A northern California police officer assigned to the vice squad told me privately that homosexual crimes in San Francisco (where society is more lenient than in any city in America) have "doubled in the last three years." "Over 40 percent of all violent crimes in San Francisco involve homosexuals." If that is true, their violent crime rate must be five or six times that of the straight community. Some of the stories this veteran crime investigator describes are too horrible to include in this book.

Now do you understand why I say that legalizing homosexuality is dangerous? If our society begins to indulge this sinful life style and homosexuals double in the next decade, so will their violent crimes. Homosexuality is not only an unhappy way of life, but it produces misery for its victims, many of whom are innocent. One six-year-old boy was recently violated and killed by a thirty-four-year-old homosexual; all the boy did was go to school that day.

5. A homosexually lenient society will incur the wrath of God.

Space does not permit us to warn of the dangers to the family that a relaxed attitude toward homosexuality will cause, but it is already a tremendous cause of family heartache and broken dreams. Nor can we detail the dangers of their increasing influence in the media, fashion, or business in general, while industry is just beginning to aim their products at these "ten million potential customers." One of the nation's leading film producers has earmarked $200,000 for advertising and promotion "aimed directly at the homosexual market." Another important danger we don't have space to consider properly is the alarming influence homosexuals increasingly have over governmental leaders who make our local and national laws. Many of these politicians are not homosexual or personally favorable to them, but for fear of being voted out of office, they pass laws seeking homosexual approbation. Usually anything favorable to the homosexual community is harmful to society in general. Some people believe that an international network of homosexuals has been working its way into governments for years. Such individuals subscribe to the plans of the internationalists and really work for their best interest rather than for the country that pays their salary. As dangerous as that could conceivably be, it is not our greatest threat.

The danger we should fear most is incurring the wrath of God on our nation. America has been mightily blessed of God. Anyone who has traveled as I have in over forty-five countries of the world can certainly see that. No other country even comes close to this nation in freedom or opportunity for the largest number of people. God has blessed our country, not because we are a Christian nation, but because we have practiced more biblical principles than any country in history. The day we legalize homosexuality and accept it as a normal way of life, we will cross over the line into human depravity and degeneracy, and God will "give us up" as he did the Sodomites, the Romans, and the many others whose rejection of his standard of morality caused their destruction.

The Bible says, "Righteousness exalteth a nation, but sin is a reproach to any people" (Proverbs 14:34). While it is true that the sin of the individual homosexual can be forgiven if he repents and calls on the name of the Lord Jesus Christ, historically speaking, the nation that endorses sodomy as a normal life style and accepts it officially is doomed to face the wrath of God. The mercy and grace of God seem to reach their breaking point when homosexuality becomes normal. Put another way, when sodomy fills the national cup of man's abominations to overflowing, God earmarks that nation for destruction.

CHAPTER THIRTEEN

An Ominous Prediction

It doesn't take a prophet or the son of a prophet to foresee what lies ahead for this country and the rest of the world. Most Bible prophecy scholars teach that we are either in "the last days," predicted in the Scriptures, or we are very close to them. Interestingly enough, homosexuality is to be a part of the buildup of the "perilously evil times" that are prophesied for the last days.

In 2 Timothy 3 we find a list delineating nineteen characteristics of the "last days." People are to be "without natural affection, unholy, despisers of those that are good, traitors, lovers of pleasures more than lovers of God." "Without natural affection" refers to sexual perversion: homosexuality.

Our Lord had a great deal to say about the last days. He compared it morally to the days of Sodom and the time just prior to the Flood, the two morally degenerate periods of history when men became so corrupt that God destroyed them. "As it was in the days of Noah . . , as it was in the days of Lot , . thus shall it be in the day when the Son of man is revealed" (Luke 17:26-30). We know that Sodom was destroyed because the inhabitants disobeyed God and perverted their sex drive with "sodomy." Although it isn't

known for sure, many Bible scholars think one of the major
sins that brought on the Flood was homosexuality.

In other words, as we approach the end of the age and the
return of Christ, we can expect that homosexuality, among
other degenerating sin practices, will increase. In fact,
Daniel 11:37 contains an interesting prediction about the
anti-Christ, who is destined to rule the world just prior to our
Lord's return to set up his Kingdom. "Neither shall he regard
the God of his fathers, *nor the desire of women . . . .*" This
suggests that the anti-Christ *may* be a homosexual. If he is,
that would explain the significance of the influential group
of international homosexuals who are rumored to be gaining
worldwide political influence.

While the sexual direction of the anti-Christ is highly
speculative, there is no question that as the age of lawlessness
approaches, homosexuality will increase until it reaches the
proportions it attained in Sodom and Gomorrah. This will
probably be a worldwide trend that will bypass only those
areas where religious or cultural principles oppose it.

Is America Doomed
to Homosexuality?

At the instigation of the pro-homosexual media, public
schools, politicians in high places, and gay militants, the tidal
wave of homosexuality that has reached enormous proportions
today threatens the very existence of a moral America. A
small but vocal minority is about to impose its will on the
silent and inactive majority. Many Christians have the false
notion that such immorality is inevitable. Somehow the
prophecies of "perilous times" for the last days have
immobilized the Christian community at a crucial time in
history when we are the last hope for a sexually sane and moral
America. It doesn't have to be that way!

God can yet save America from this onslaught of

perversion, but it will take the participation of the fifty million Americans who claim to be "born again." If we do nothing, our culture is lost. As God would have saved Sodom from destruction for "ten righteous souls," so he can rescue America if we bestir ourselves and use our freedoms wisely.

What Can Be Done?

1. Write letters to local state and national leaders opposing any further leniency toward homosexuality.

2. Vigorously campaign to elect Christians to public office. Former California Assemblyman E. Richard Barnes, my personal friend and a former Navy chaplain, successfully fought single-handedly against the homosexual consenting law for ten years in our state. Immediately after his defeat when he was no longer in the Capitol to warn against it, the Senate passed the laws by one vote. Just one more Christian in the California Senate would have turned back the tidal wave one more time. Instead, one too few gave it momentum. We need more men and women like Dick Barnes in Sacramento, Lansing, Columbus, and Washingon, D.C.

3. Energetically campaign to protect American school children legally from homosexual teachers.

The Realities of Politics

The silent majority does not run this country. We have been manipulated for years by self-seeking politicians, minority pressure groups, secular humanists, the sex entertainment industry, and other anti-Christian and anti-American forces that make up no more than 20 to 25 percent of our population. Most Americans want a moral society. That is clearly evidenced by the January 1978 results of *Good Housekeeping's* ninth annual poll on "The Ten Most Admired Women." First place went to *Anita Bryant*! After all the ridicule, misrepresentation, and abuse to which she has been subjected by the media, American women still proclaim her the most admired woman in the world. That is the female voice of the silent majority. It is time for us Christians to lead this enormous majority of pro-moral Americans in reestablishing the values that earned for us the blessings of God on our country.

The Future of America

What is the future of our country morally? It could go either way. We could follow the route of homosexual corruption as destined for the rest of the world, or we could shake ourselves from lethargy and use our freedoms to save our freedom. Edmund Burke sagely commented, "All that is necessary for evil to triumph is that good men do nothing." What is the future of America? It is entirely up to you!

Notes

[1] Del Hood, "Gays Fight Long-Held Traditions," *El Cajon-Californian*, June 3, 1976, p. 1.

[2] Del Hood, "Changes Being Urged for Gay Rights," *El Cajon-Californian*, June 4, 1976, p. 1.

[3] *Ibid*.

[4] William D. Rodgers, *The Gay Invasion* (Denver: Accent Books, 1977), p. 31.

[5] *Ibid*., p. 33.

[6] *Ibid*., p. 34.

[7] *Ibid*., p. 37.

[8] C. A. Tripp, *The Homosexual Matrix* (New York: New American Library, 1975), p. 5.

[9] "The State of the Language 1977," *Time*, January 2, 1978, p. 36.

[10] Murray Norris, *Christian Family Renewal Newsletter*, Box 73, Clovis, California.

[11] John White, *Eros Defiled* (Downers Grove, Ill.: InterVarsity Press, 1977), p. 119.

[12] Murray Norris, "There's Nothing Gay About Homosexuality," *Christian Family Renewal Newsletter*, Box 73, Clovis, California.

[13] Alan Ebert, *The Homosexuals*, (New York: Macmillan, Inc., 1977), p. 324.

[14] *Ibid*., p. 275.

[15] *Ibid*., p. 330.

[16] *Ibid*., pp. 309, 310.

[17] Daniel Cappon, *Toward an Understanding of Homosexuality* (Englewood Cliffs, N. J., Prentice-Hall, Inc., 1965), n.p.

[18] Tripp, p. 10.

[19] *Ibid*., p. 11.

[20] Tripp, p. 16.

[21] James D. Mallory, "A Psychiatrist's View of Homosexuality," *Christian Life*, October, 1977, p. 28.

[22] Irving Bieber, *Homosexuality: A Psychoanalytic Study of Male Homosexuals* (New York: Basic Books, Inc., 1962), n.p.

[23] Tripp, p. 77.

[24] *Ibid*.

[25] White, p. 111.

[26] Tripp, p. 82.

[27] Oliver J. Siemans and William W. Halcomb, *Sex Wrong Side Out*, P.O. Box 1202, San Clemente, California 92672, pp. 10, 11.

[28] Used by permission of the publisher, Fleming H. Revell, (copyright © 1977).

[29] Rodgers, p. 106.

[30] *Ibid*., p. 99.

[31] *Ibid*., p. 101.

[32] *Ibid*., p. 103.

[33] *Ibid*., p. 104.

[34] Anita Bryant, *The Anita Bryant Story*, Revell Publishing Co., p. 125.

[35] "Carter Names Lesbian in Political Payoff?" *Spotlight*, August 1, 1977.

[36] *National Enquirer*, June 7, 1977.